Lessons from Nehemiah

Ted Murray

Scripture Truth Publications

LESSONS FROM NEHEMIAH

First published as articles in the magazine "Scripture Truth" 2004-08
FIRST EDITION
FIRST PUBLISHED August 2008
ISBN: 978-0-901860-86-6
Copyright © 2008 Scripture Truth Publications

All rights reserved. No part of this publication may be reproduced, stored in a retrieval system, or transmitted, in any form or by any means, electronic, mechanical, photocopying, recording or otherwise without prior permission of Scripture Truth Publications.

Scripture quotations, unless otherwise indicated, are taken from the New King James Version®. Copyright © 1982 by Thomas Nelson, Inc. Used by permission. All rights reserved.

Scripture quotations marked (NIV) are taken from the HOLY BIBLE, NEW INTERNATIONAL VERSION. Copyright © 1973, 1978, 1984, International Bible Society. Used by permission of Hodder & Stoughton Publishers, a member of the Hodder Headline Group. All rights reserved. "NIV" is a registered trademark of International Bible Society. UK trademark number 1448790.

Scripture quotations marked (AV) are taken from The Authorized (King James) Version. Rights in the Authorized Version are vested in the Crown. Reproduced by permission of the Crown's patentee, Cambridge University Press.

Cover photograph ©iStockphoto.com/alexsl (Alex Slobodkin)

Published by Scripture Truth Publications
31-33 Glover Street,
Crewe, Cheshire, CW1 3LD

Scripture Truth is an imprint of Central Bible Hammond Trust, a charitable trust

Typesetting by John Rice
Printed by Lightning Source

CONTENTS

Introduction 5
1. Nehemiah – the troubled man (chapter 1) 7
2. Nehemiah – the daring man (chapter 2:1-11) . 12
3. Nehemiah – the inspector (chapter 2:11-20) ... 19
4. The repairers (chapter 3) 26
5. A mind to work (chapter 4) 34
6. Problems with the people (chapter 5) 42
7. A personal attack (chapter 6) 49
8. Restoration (chapter 7) 56
9. Renewal (chapter 8:1-12) 63
10. Obedience and refreshing (chapter 8:13-18) .. 71
11. Repentant prayer (chapter 9) 79
12. A new beginning (chapters 10 & 11) 88
13. A dedication parade (chapter 12) 97
14. Beware lest you fall (chapter 13) 105
Appendix: Nehemiah's prayers 113

LESSONS FROM NEHEMIAH

Introduction

Nehemiah is introduced to us as the man who succeeds Ezra. His book is the sequel to Ezra and, for a long time, was reckoned as the second part of the one book. The division of the Hebrew Scriptures was only made in the 16th century. The Hebrew Bible of Daniel Bomberg, printed in Venice in 1535, was the first to show a division of the two books. The Geneva Bible (1560) also shows separate books.

The book tells of events that occurred between the years 445-432 BC, approximately. It brings before us not only a man with a mission but also a man concerned about the well being of his brethren. His mission was to bring security to his brethren and a return to living in accordance with God's word.

Some 10 years after the commencement of Ezra's work, there was considerable opposition to the rebuilding of the walls of Jerusalem (see Ezra 4:7-24). As a result, the walls of Jerusalem were completely razed, the doors broken down and burned, and the people suffered further persecution. It was this sorry scene that was presented to Nehemiah as the book opens. Little wonder that he was deeply troubled!

Breakdown was very evident. The people of God were demoralised; the testimony was in disarray. There were, however, a few who were very concerned about the state of affairs and were prepared to do something about it. Today, as we look around us in Christendom, we are also troubled by the state of things. The testimony to Christ, of which we are a part, is in disarray. The authority of God's word is being set aside in favour of more politically correct opinions. Infighting and intrigue are prevalent amongst the people of God, resulting in abject weakness and a decline in numbers. Is it sufficient to say to ourselves, "It is a day of small things. We should be satisfied with the things that remain."? Or should we, like Nehemiah of old, be concerned and be people with a mission?

1.
Nehemiah – the troubled man

CHAPTER 1

NEHEMIAH'S SAD NEWS

The chapter opens by giving Nehemiah's credentials. It then briefly describes a visit to Nehemiah by his brother, Hanani, and some of the men from Judea. In Hebrew, Nehemiah means 'Jehovah is comfort' and Hanani means 'gracious'. Hanani was, as we can see, a man who was concerned about two problems: he had a care for his brother's welfare; he was also concerned about the situation in Jerusalem. In fact, we see here both an individual and a collective care for the welfare of the people who had been left in Jerusalem, exposed to all manner of influences from around as well as from within.

These men could have had their prayer meeting in Jerusalem and left the situation with the Lord. They, however, went a step further. They went to see Nehemiah, a man who had the wherewithal to do something about their situation. What an example they are for the assemblies of today. There are times when the solution to a problem is in the realms of our ability and our resources but, because of pride, prejudice and selfishness, we avoid these means of solving our problems.

From the result of the meeting with Nehemiah, it would appear that the visitors kept nothing back. They did not put on a brave face; they stated the naked truth. Things were desperate. The people who were left in Jerusalem were in great distress – they suffered reproach from all around and had no security.

The times in which we live are not so different from those of Nehemiah's day. This country has turned its back on Christianity. Attempts are being made to do away with a daily Christian service or assembly in our schools. If the school is a church school, then the governors can retain the right to hold a time of worship. Humanism is taught as part of comparative religious studies. The children are to know about, but not be taught, Christianity. In church life, too, the world has made its inroads, influencing attitudes, manners and deportment. The walls and gates, as it were, are in ruins, and we see the consequences.

The problem is that many of us are unaware of the situation in which we find ourselves. It is prevalent in our lives as individuals and also in our relationships with those with whom we claim to be in practical Christian fellowship, yet we disregard their concerns in matters of testimony and association.

Nehemiah's prayer (verses 4-7)

Nehemiah is deeply affected by the sad news he receives. He sits down, reflects on what he has heard, then weeps and prays, as did Ezra before him, to "the God of heaven" (verse 4). He realises that God's throne was no longer on earth but removed to heaven and that God's influence had been cast aside. In deep humiliation, he confesses his sin and that of the people. "We have sinned against Thee: both I and my father's house have sinned" (verse 6, AV), he cries. He goes a step further stating, "We have acted very wickedly" (verse 7, NIV). Nehemiah was deeply moved by the conditions of the breakdown.

Nehemiah's attitude is in marked contrast to the Pharisaic attitude which is sometimes seen in the assembly today. Many of us are aware of the breakdown. We are apt to wring our hands, lamenting that things are in a poor condition. But we are not prepared to admit that these conditions are the result of our failure to maintain the testimony which has been passed down by faithful men of God in past generations. When was the last time that we used words similar to Nehemiah's and accepted that we have sinned and acted corruptly?

Nehemiah's faith (verses 8-11)

Just as we have seen the contrition of Nehemiah, so also we see his faith. These two attributes seem to go hand in hand. Ezra (see Ezra 9) and Daniel (see Daniel 9) were men who acted similarly. Now Nehemiah goes on to remind God of His own words: "Remember, I pray, the word that You commanded Your servant Moses" (see Leviticus 26:40-45; Deuteronomy 4:23; 30:1-6). Even if, because of their transgressions, His people had been scattered into a stranger's land, God had promised that, if they repented, He would bring them back to the place which He had chosen for them. This was the place where God had chosen "to set His name there" (AV), a place where He was to be honoured and worshipped.

We now see the selfless side of Nehemiah. When approaching God in repentance, he involved himself, his family and the people. But now, as he asks for blessing, it is for these, "Your servants and Your people" (verse 10).

Those people were His redeemed. They had experienced the great power of God, not only in their deliverance from the bondage of Egypt, but also from the bondage of Babylon.

This surely reminds us of our Lord Jesus Christ and His prayer in John 17. There He prays for His own who are in the world "that they may behold My glory" (John 17:24). What a contrast from the ruin all around – to see His glory, to be occupied with that which is His by right! What a joy that will be in that day when we see Him as He is (1 John 3:2)! But what about today, the day in which we live? How much time do we devote to dwelling on the moral, personal, redemptive and official glories of the Lord Jesus Christ? Remember, He is Lord of all!

What comfort it must have been to Nehemiah as he reminded himself before God of that great work that God had done for the nation. By faith, Nehemiah was expecting great and mighty acts by God once more. Only when Nehemiah has made intercession for the people, "Your servants who desire to fear Your name", do we find him pleading for mercy for himself. Nehemiah was cupbearer to the great and mighty potentate, Artaxerxes, who, at a whim, took the lives of men and women who failed to please him. Yet Nehemiah calls him "this man" (verse 11)! Artaxerxes was a man of little consequence in comparison to the mighty God in whom Nehemiah trusted! We, too, should take heart when the fear of men takes hold of our lives. Then we need to remind ourselves of the Lord's servant, Nehemiah, and others like him down the pages of history, who, although giving due respect to the position that God gives to rulers, realised that the Lord is in overall control.

It seems as if Nehemiah has already made up his mind as to what his plan of action is to be. Knowing the power of the king, he asks the Lord to prosper this day and to grant mercy in the sight of "this man". Chapter 2 declares how Nehemiah's request was granted. Nehemiah prayed in faith. We, too, should remember when we pray that we exercise faith in our great, omnipotent and compassionate Lord. Let us keep this in mind as we keep on praying!

2.
Nehemiah – the daring man
CHAPTER 2:1-11

WAITING ON GOD

Thirteen years have transpired since Ezra left Babylon for Jerusalem to carry out his task of retrieving the situation there for the Lord. We saw in chapter 1 that there appeared to have been another falling away in the testimony of the remnant in Jerusalem. Four months have passed during which Nehemiah ponders the news received from Jerusalem.

As chapter 2 opens, we find Nehemiah still doing his duty in the king's palace. He was waiting for an opportunity when he could approach "this man" (1:11) concerning the welfare of his brethren in Jerusalem, but was very conscious of the danger in which he could find himself. He was the king's cupbearer, the man who tasted the wine to check its suitability and so ensure that there was nothing in it that would harm the king. He would have been a man of integrity, a man to whose counsel the king would listen, a dependable man. Here we find him summoning up courage, patiently waiting for the opportune moment when he might ask the king for permission to leave his presence.

There are times when patience has to be exercised while we wait for the moment when the Lord chooses to act. We are quite happy to sing the words

> *"Our times are in Thy hand,*
> *Whatever they may be,*
> *Pleasing or painful, dark or bright,*
> *As best may seem to Thee."*

But very often it is another matter to experience the darkness and the pain. Nehemiah was passing through both these experiences as he waited on the king, but he was not deterred from his task. For four whole months he had thought about this problem. During that time, nothing seemed to be happening that would resolve the matter. Those earnest prayers seemed to have gone unanswered. No wonder he was looking down in the mouth, even in the king's presence. What a situation to be in!

SEIZING THE OPPORTUNITY

Nehemiah must have felt helpless but he was certainly not hopeless. When the king asked why he looked so sad, he was able to grasp, with both hands as it were, the opportunity that the Lord gave him. There are times when circumstances today cause the Christian to be downcast, when God-given opportunities to serve Him slip by. It has been said that "an opportunity neglected can result in an eternity lost". What virtues we find in Nehemiah. Scripture records that he was dreadfully afraid (verse 2) as he heard the king say, "There is nothing physically wrong with you, but there is something on your heart". In Nehemiah's answer, we hear the truth and see an example of courage.

To speak the truth in any circumstance can require courage. To stand for the truth requires daring and fortitude. These virtues are in short supply in today's world, but they should readily be seen amongst believers. In Nehemiah, we see a man who was waiting for the God-given moment and, in his response, we have a pattern which we should follow.

Nehemiah shows his respect for the king and informs him of the reason for his sadness. He tells the king of his awareness of the sad situation in his homeland and expresses his concern for his people there. Are we fully aware of the sad situation in Christendom? Do we sorrow for, and with, those who suffer for the sake of the testimony of Christ? Or are we satisfied with our lot? Nehemiah had a reasonably secure position. He was, as stated previously, in a position of trust. His job security was good, provided he did nothing to upset the king. He had a roof over his head; he fed from the king's table.

Nehemiah's general circumstances were not so very different from those of many of us today. The Government has established a welfare system which, in the main, looks after our physical needs from the cradle to the grave. In the west, we know very little about hardship or the persecution suffered by fellow believers in other countries. We ought daily to thank God for the material blessings that we are inclined to take for granted and for the fact that we are kept from persecution. But we must also bring to Him at the throne of grace the needs of our suffering fellow believers: "And if one member suffers, all the members suffer with it" (1 Corinthians 12:26).

Nehemiah realises that the moment for which he had been waiting had now come. The king asks, "What do you request?" What a moment this was for Nehemiah! He was given the opportunity to make his request to a potentate who had all the necessary resources! But we read that Nehemiah first prays "to the God of heaven" (verse 4) and then speaks to the king. Note the order we find in Scripture. God is given the pre-eminent position. Paul reminds us that this position of pre-eminence belongs to the Lord by right (Colossians 1:18).

Nehemiah's prayer was from the heart; it was direct, not wordy. Nehemiah did not wait to attend the prayer meeting or for his prayer time, but an immediate cry for help went from his heart. And God heard his cry! Nehemiah not only walked, but also talked, with his God.

We now find Nehemiah, confident that God was with him, making his request to rebuild his homeland. To the casual reader, this might seem a rather audacious and improbable request to make. But to a man who had absolute confidence in his God, it was not so. The Lord Jesus reminds us that, with God, all things are possible (Matthew 19:26). All the thoughts, desires and plans which Nehemiah had had during those four long months were now unfolded before the king and his queen. Nehemiah does not appear to have been tongue-tied, or to need time to make his presentation to the king. He straightway embarks on the need of the project. God had made Nehemiah aware of the breakdown, the conditions and the lack of materials. And God had put the desire in Nehemiah's heart to rebuild.

We can see the breakdown in the testimony today; we know the conditions which exist in many assemblies. We may moan about the lack of resources, but often the desire to rebuild is also lacking. Let us never forget that we have access to the King of kings, the Head of His Body, the Church. He is the One who has untold resources, the One who delights to give, the One who has said, "Ask and you will receive" (John 16:24). Do we know what it is to tap into those unlimited resources?

Nehemiah did not just ask for leave of absence from the court for a period of time. He also asked for a letter of commendation, a permit to pass through the region beyond the river, and an order to Asaph to make available all the timber Nehemiah required for the repairs of the gates and to build a dwelling place for Nehemiah (verse 8). The verse goes on to read, "the king granted them to me according to the good hand of my God upon me". Like Ezra before him, Nehemiah acknowledges that all blessing comes from God. So Paul reminds us that it is God who gives the increase (1 Corinthians 3:6).

READY TO HELP

We are not told how long it took for Nehemiah to organise his retinue. As an official of the king's court, he had a standing amongst the people of his day and the king gave him an escort. He does not appear to have wasted any time: "Then I went to the governors beyond the river…" (verse 9). We are apt to consider what may be the most favourable time, whether the most up to date equipment is at our disposal, whether we have met current criteria regarding safety in the workplace, etc.

Nehemiah does not appear to have any such worries. He was armed with a letter of authority from the king. He was on the king's business! We ought to remind ourselves that this, too, is our task today. We are on the King's business! We have His commission to spread His word. We have His request to remember Him. In the New Testament, we have His instructions, the apostles' doctrine, and we have the indwelling of His Holy Spirit. But there are times when we still lack that determination to fulfil His work.

The daunting journey over, Nehemiah now presents his credentials to the governors of the mixed race of Samaritans, who had been settled in the land at the command of Esar-haddon. He meets two somewhat disturbed men, Sanballat and Tobiah, one a Horonite and the other an Ammonite, descendants of Lot. Both of these men were the result of the shameful events recorded in Genesis 19, when God was left out of the equation and man, or more particularly women, took control.

From this event, we learn that when someone seeks the welfare of God's people, there will always be opposition. Initially Sanballat and Tobiah were merely disturbed by Nehemiah's presence. Later in the book, we see that their agitation turned to mockery, then contempt, then conspiracy, and finally, direct opposition to Nehemiah. Satan has not dramatically changed his tactics. They are still used today by those who oppose the Gospel. In the west, mercifully, we are often only exposed to his less severe opposition. Nevertheless, it is sad to see in the church today those who attempt to pour cold water on any movement of the Spirit of God. Deuteronomy 23:3-6 states: "An Ammonite or a Moabite shall not enter into the assembly of the LORD". This judgment was the direct result of the failure of these peoples to help the children of Israel in the wilderness, of their hiring Balaam to curse the Israelites, and of their leading the Israelites into idolatry.

There are, sadly, some in assemblies today who are embracing customs which are contrary to Scripture, gladly adopting practices which are current in present day Christendom, scorning those who hold fast to the principles and teaching which were graciously restored by the Lord, and have been passed down to us by men of God in past generations. Just before he was martyred, Paul asked Timothy to bring with him the cloak, the books and, especially, the parchments (2 Timothy 4:13). Today, there seems to be a tendency to neglect the comfort of the cloak of fellowship, to ignore the scriptures which do not comply with current modern thinking, and to let the teachings contained in the writings of saints of God gather dust on our bookshelves.

3.
Nehemiah – the inspector

CHAPTER 2:11-20

HIS ARRIVAL IN JERUSALEM

We now find Nehemiah having a rest, but only for three days (verse 11). But the man of action was not content to sit on his laurels as the visitor from the palace. No doubt, many of the notables in Jerusalem would want to catch up on the news of the court; many would want news of their relations who remained in Babylon. Others would just wish to pass the time of day with their notable visitor.

For his part, Nehemiah would ask pertinent questions about the state of affairs in the city. Why had the rebuilding work stopped? Are the daily sacrifices being continued? Are the gatekeepers still carrying out their duties? What about the priests and Levites? There would be all sorts of answers to these questions. Some would alarm him; some would placate his fears. Some would confirm what he had been told in Shushan, but all would make him keener to see the conditions for himself. God had given him a job to do. He had been granted permission to come to Jerusalem and he had the necessary paperwork to obtain building materials. He knew that he was in the place, and in the position, that God had for him. He had circumstantial evidence that what he was undertaking was in accord with God's will. All this was the outcome of that brief prayer in 2:4.

As we think about these verses, we should be encouraged as we see how God not only answered Nehemiah's prayer, but placed him in a position of authority with all the resources necessary to complete the task which God had laid upon his heart. In our day, too, when the Lord gives us a job to do, we can be assured that He will also give us the wherewithal to do it. The Lord is no man's debtor!

JERUSALEM BY NIGHT

Having no doubt heard the various leaders, each giving differing views of the conditions of the city, Nehemiah could not contain the burden that was his any longer. By night, he decides to see the ruined conditions for himself. He did not share the burden that God had laid upon his heart with anyone else (verse 16). He did not broadcast his intentions in order to seek assistance or to put anyone under duress to assist him in his fact-finding inspection of the walls and gates of Jerusalem. It was Nehemiah's exercise, and his alone, that God had laid on his heart. We see in this action the example of a man who was circumspect in word and deed. Nehemiah did not boast or gossip about the task before him. He had already experienced the good hand of God upon him in the palace, and on the journey. So he was confident that God would enable him to fulfil the task he had been given.

We are reminded of God's promise to Joshua: "Have I not commanded you? Be strong and of good courage; do not be afraid, nor be dismayed, for the LORD your God is with you wherever you go" (Joshua 1:9). As we proceed through this book, we shall see how Nehemiah proves this verse for himself. In Nehemiah, we have yet another example of how to proceed when the Lord has laid a task on one's heart. By telling no one of his task, he did not have to hear the whys and wherefores from people who had other ideas, e.g. is it the right time? are there sufficient funds to take on such an enormous task? One has written, "When the Lord distinctly gives a task to any one of His servants, nothing is frequently more dangerous than consultation with others" (Edward Dennett). Once discussions are held about that which the Lord has so forcibly laid on His servant, then faith starts to take a back seat under the weight of prudence and so-called common sense. It is only when the time is right for the execution of the task, then and only then, does Nehemiah invite help from others.

FINDING OUT THE FACTS

It is difficult to discover the full extent of Nehemiah's fact-finding tour of the walls. He leaves the city by the Valley Gate, dropping down into the Tyropoeon Valley. From there, he was able to see the extent of the damage to the long length of wall that had once protected the western side of the city of David. He then makes his way to the Fountain Gate, passing by the Dung Gate, on the way to the southernmost point of the wall. He then turns northward, up the Kidron valley, to see the damage to the eastern side of the wall. Proceeding along this eastern side of the wall, he would eventually come to the northernmost part of the wall. This part, which incorporated the Fish Gate, also enclosed part of the Temple Mount. Nehemiah finally arrives back to his starting point, the Valley Gate.

In thinking about this tour by night, there are a number of issues on which to focus. The wall surrounding the City of David, the area of the city where the general citizens lived, would suggest his concern for the welfare of the people of God. That part of the wall surrounding the Temple Mount would suggest Nehemiah's concern for the worship of God. The Ophel, being the area where the priests and Levites dwelt, suggests concern for the servants of God. So Nehemiah's night time tour challenges us today about our concern for the following:

- The state of the general testimony

- The welfare of those with whom we are in fellowship

- The needs of God's servants

- How we come together for the Lord's Supper and for worship of the Father

- Is our worship in the power of the Holy Spirit?

Nehemiah's exercise concerning his beloved Jerusalem was personal and God-given. In our day, concern about the state of the breakdown must start with individual exercise before God, so that we are fully aware of the situation in which we find ourselves. What Nehemiah saw was exactly what he had heard (compare verse 13; 1:3). There had been neither embellishment nor understatement of the situation in the report given to him. How do we convey our local conditions to other interested believers? Are we totally honest with the truth, or do we put a slight gloss on things? We, too, need to tell of conditions as they really are. Otherwise visitors, or other believers who move into the district, will find that our local conditions differ from what they had been led to believe.

NEHEMIAH – THE INSPECTOR

THE INSPECTOR'S REPORT

What a scene is now before us! We can try to imagine the assembled company. The leaders of Jerusalem, the priestly hierarchy and the ordinary citizens gathered together in Nehemiah's lodgings. He does not berate the assembled company for their failure to repair the walls but identifies himself with their distress: "You see the distress that we are in, how Jerusalem lies waste, and its gates are burned with fire. Come and let us build the wall of Jerusalem, that we may no longer be a reproach" (verse 17). Nehemiah makes them fully aware that he has firsthand experience of the conditions of the walls and gates.

He does not, however, wring his hands asking what can be done! He takes the opportunity to tell them how he had been blessed by God. He had personal experience of the good hand of God upon him (verse 18). He knew of God's overriding, providential care during his long journey to Jerusalem. He could relate how the king had given him leave from his duties at the palace, together with permission to source the materials he needed to repair the breakdown and also to provide for his own domestic situation. Materially, Nehemiah appears to be well provided for, but he does not emphasise this point. He rather testifies that "the hand of my God" was in it all. What a wonderful way in which to encourage a distressed, downcast company of people! We, today, should also not be ashamed of telling what the Lord has done for us. We should recount humbly, without boasting, how God has worked in our lives. In this way, we, too, can encourage, cheer and motivate the disheartened amongst us.

Having given his report, and testified of his experience of God's hand upon him, Nehemiah invites the people to join him in his task of rebuilding the walls: "Come and let us build" (verse 17). Nehemiah must have been encouraged by the resolute response of this believing, cheered company: "Let us rise up and build" (verse 18). This was not idle talk, for we read, "They set their hands to do this good work" (verse 18). God always has ready hands to do what is according to His will.

OPPOSITION TO THE WORK

Whenever there is a work of God in progress, Satan will oppose it. We see this as we read again of Sanballat and Tobiah. This time they have another companion, Geshem the Arab. The former two had been deeply disturbed when Nehemiah first came to Jerusalem (verse 10). Now we read that they laugh and pour scorn on Nehemiah's decision to rebuild the walls and gates. We live in a day where we, too, may be laughed at for our beliefs because they are based on Scripture. Geshem, a descendant of Ishmael or Esau, typifies what is of the flesh. We see around us in Christendom the effects of this tendency: acts of adultery, divorce and homosexuality are not only being condoned but are now being accepted as a way of life. This manner of life is an abomination to God and contrary to His word.

The walls are indeed in ruins! They are completely broken down and the enemy has free access within, pouring scorn on those who are walking faithfully before God, in accordance with His word. What a lesson we can learn from Nehemiah's response to their mockery and their accusation of being rebellious to the king! Nehemiah confesses to them his unwavering faith in God. "The God of heaven Himself will prosper us; therefore we His servants will arise and build, but you have no heritage or right or memorial in Jerusalem" (verse 20).

The boldness and confidence of Nehemiah shine out like a ray of sunlight on a gloomy day. The combination of his experience of, and his faith in, God are evident in this reply. Today, we all have had some experience of the way in which the Lord has helped us in the past. Like Nehemiah, we should trust Him for the future. Our stand for Christ should be similarly bold and confident in this day of mockery and scorn. James reminds us, "Resist the devil and he will flee from you" (James 4:7). So Paul can exclaim to the Romans, "If God is for us, who can be against us?" (Romans 8:31). With the added assurance of these scriptures, let us be bold and confident, rather than apologetic, in the face of those who are bringing evil into the Church. We need to rebuild the walls of separation from such evil. Evil practitioners have "no heritage or right or memorial" in the Church of the living God.

4.
The repairers
CHAPTER 3

INTRODUCTION

Nehemiah had seen the destruction of Jerusalem at firsthand, but had encouraged its inhabitants by his personal testimony of the good hand of God upon him. Ignoring the mockery of the opposition, Nehemiah had obtained agreement that the city walls should be rebuilt. Now he puts the citizens of Jerusalem to the test. Word goes out for volunteers to repair the city wall!

THE PEOPLE WHO WORKED

Nehemiah did not ask for a c.v. from any of these volunteers, nor did he appear to want to interview them to assess their suitability for the work. If he had, many of those listed in this chapter would have been deemed quite unsuitable! What a mixture of professions! Goldsmiths, perfumers, priests, Levites, agricultural workers and women are listed amongst those who took on the task. The church today is a similar mixture of people, with differing skills and temperaments, all of which, when freely offered, can be used by God for the rebuilding of the Christian testimony and the furtherance of the Gospel.

There are a number of interesting lessons for us today in this list of names and places in chapter 3. At first sight, the chapter may appear to be simply a list of words, which many of us have difficulty in pronouncing and, consequently, tend to give them a miss! However, Paul reminds Timothy, "All scripture is given by inspiration of God, and is profitable for doctrine, for reproof, for correction, for instruction in righteousness, that the man of God may be complete, thoroughly equipped for every good work" (2 Timothy 3:16-17). We do well, then, to look into the meanings of these names. Certainly, in Old Testament times, babies were given names whose meanings reflected an immediate significance, e.g. Samuel: heard of God, or highlighted some future significant event, e.g. Gideon: the cutter down.

The list in this chapter contains some 39 names of those directly involved in the rebuilding of the wall, as well as 31 of their fathers and 3 of their grandfathers. Also named are 8 groups of people who were collectively involved in the repairs to the wall. Amongst the repairers are listed 8 individual names with no apparent family backing. This surely tells us that in the work of God today there similarly is room for individuals, room for those with family backing and room for groups of believers.

Of the names listed, 11 include the name of Jehovah in their meanings. In these 11, a progression can be seen, commencing with Jehoida (verse 6), meaning 'Jehovah has adorned', through to Shemaiah (verse 29), meaning 'Jehovah has heard'. So we see in these names how the Lord provides for us in all our needs and circumstances – from the moment when, by grace, we were given that new robe of righteousness, to the end of our life here on earth, recognising His answering grace to all our needs.

Another point of note is the meaning of the first and last names in this list. The first name, Eliashib, means 'God will restore'. What comfort can be obtained from that promise, as much in our day as it would have been in Nehemiah's day! How encouraging this promise is to our faith as we look at the breakdown that surrounds the church today. We can have the assurance that our Lord God has the ability to restore! The last name mentioned in the list, Malchijah, means 'The LORD is King'. This ought to remind us that our Saviour is the King of kings. He is the Sovereign Lord at whose name every knee must bow and every tongue confess that He is Lord (Philippians 2:10-11).

Other names give what appear to be characteristic details of those involved in the work, e.g. Rephaiah means 'healed of Jehovah'. One name, Bavai, meaning 'my goings', is of Persian origin. Its inclusion shows how even those of independent tendencies can be accommodated in the repairs of the walls.

Several names have some form of commendation attached. A similar feature is found in Romans 16 where the apostle Paul mentions those who worked earnestly or diligently for the Lord. So we read in this chapter: "Baruch the son of Zabbai carefully repaired the other section…" (verse 20).

In this chapter, we see those who worked as individuals – Meshullam worked by his lodgings (verse 30). Here we see one who was concerned about the security of his home. Are we today concerned about the security of our homes from worldly influences? We may spend large sums of money ensuring the physical security of our homes but are we equally concerned about their spiritual security?

Several worked together as groups: "And after him the priests, the men of the plain, made repairs" (verse 22). Manual work may not have been to their liking; they may have had differing concepts as to how to carry out the work – but they worked together for the furtherance of the cause.

Sadly, there are also those who were not prepared to put their backs into the work: "…the Tekoites made repairs; but their nobles did not put their shoulders to the work of their Lord" (verse 5). The Lord solemnly notes what is not done for Himself: "Assuredly, I say to you, inasmuch as you did not do it to one of the least of these, you did not do it to Me" (Matthew 25:45). But equally, the Lord misses nothing that is done for Himself: "Inasmuch as you did it to one of the least of these My brethren, you did it to Me" (Matthew 25:40). So it is recorded here that, although their nobles might refuse to work, the common people of Tekoa rebuilt two sections (verses 5, 27).

Today, there is a tendency to think that, because numbers are small, we should go and join up with a larger group. Invariably this means that principles, which were once held dear, are compromised or given up altogether. If this had been the case in Nehemiah's day, then the walls would have remained derelict and the means of protection and separation would have been totally ineffective – only 39 repairers, together with the daughters of one of them, are mentioned in this chapter. What were so few faced with such great need?

Separated unto God

Moses claimed a special place for himself and the children of Israel before God: "For wherein shall it be known here that I and thy people have found grace in thy sight? Is it not in that thou goest with us? So shall we be separated, I and thy people, from all the people that are upon the face of the earth" (Exodus 33:16, AV). The church today should occupy a similar position. In Nehemiah 3, this forgotten truth was about to be reclaimed. Through the grace of God, the people were once more to be set apart for God. The rebuilt walls and gates would be a physical reminder of that fact.

In Christendom today, we see, and feel the effects of, the ruin brought in by this lack of separation. The desire to occupy the place where God would have us be needs to be stimulated. There is a great need today for men like Nehemiah, whose name means 'consolation of Jehovah'. We need men who have the God-given ability to console, stimulate, encourage and maintain the momentum of the church today.

The work that was done

As well as the names of those who were involved in the work of rebuilding, the chapter provides some interesting details regarding the work of rebuilding, with mention of the various sections of the wall completed. There are some interesting lessons for our Christian testimony to be learned from these details.

In verse 1, we read that Eliashib, the high priest, together with his brethren the priests, built up the Sheep Gate. It was important for them in their position to have easy access for the sacrificial sheep. They cleared the route, built the gate, consecrated it, and hung the doors – but omitted to fit the bolts and bars (see verse 3 for contrast).

It looked as if they had done a good job; they even extended their task to the continuation of the wall as far as the Tower of Hananeel. But here was a man, apparently a religious man, who was not fully committed to the cause. In keeping with this, we later find him making an alliance with Tobiah, one of the enemies of God's people, even to the extent of giving him a large room in the storerooms of the temple (13:4-9). Moreover, his grandson married the daughter of Sanballat the Horonite, another enemy of God's people (Nehemiah 13:28).

In Eliashib, we see a man who valued his position and, probably more so, the benefits that went with the post of high priest in Israel, but who had political connections with the enemies of the people of God. We see similar situations in the professing Church today where, not only men of high office or status, but people in general want to have their feet in both camps. We have to examine our own consciences to see whether we, too, fall into this failure. The solemn warning of James 4:4 is still very relevant today, for to be friendly with the world is to be an enemy of God.

It is also worth noting that Eliashib did not do the repairs opposite his house (see verses 20-21; contrast Benjamin and Hashub, verse 23). Paul writes to Timothy about the importance of order in the church and emphasises that this order must begin in the home: "A bishop then must be blameless, the husband of one wife, vigilant,... given to hospitality, apt to teach...one that ruleth well his own house, having his children in subjection with all gravity..." (1 Timothy 3:1-5, AV). What a challenge for us today is this aspect of Christian testimony, the need to rule well in our homes! The home is the place where we relax, and rightly so. But that same relaxation may lead us to cultivate relationships, habits and practices which cause us to compromise the truth we claim to hold.

One particular feature should be noted: "Next to him Uzziel the son of Harhaiah, one of the goldsmiths, made repairs. Also next to him Hananiah, one of the perfumers, made repairs; and they fortified Jerusalem as far as the Broad Wall" (verse 8). Here we have two professions totally unsuitable for repairing walls! The goldsmith's skill brought added attraction to ordinary objects and made things of beauty. The perfumer's skill was to attract the attention of the senses and, consequently, to enhance the wearer or the object on which the product was put. These skills were hardly suitable for working on the ruin and rubble of the walls!

There are many in the church today who consider that they lack the necessary skills for functioning in the Christian testimony. It is good to see that these two groups of workers, apparently unskilled in building practices, were ready to work and were used to good effect for the repairs and rebuilding of the walls. When we offer ourselves to the Lord for His work, it is His prerogative how He uses us. We may readily sing the words of the hymn:

> *There's a work for Jesus ready at your hand,*
> *'Tis a task the Master just for you has planned.*
> *Haste to do His bidding, yield Him service true!*
> *There's a work for Jesus none but you can do.*

And the refrain:

> *Work for Jesus day by day.*
> *Serve Him ever, falter never, Christ obey.*
> *Yield Him service loyal, true;*
> *There's a work for Jesus none but you can do!*

But we are not prepared to do some of the tasks that stare us in the face! How sad it is that the walls of Christian testimony are left in ruins when a helping hand could do the repair! The skills of these men, skills of attraction and enhancement, in a spiritual sense are just what is needed to complement the Christian testimony in the neighbourhoods where we are found.

The people in Nehemiah's day, by rebuilding the walls and gates of Jerusalem, demonstrated to the nations around that they intended to re-establish the path of separation as instructed in Exodus 33:16. Today there is still a need for that path to be re-established. We see in Christendom today different denominations. If we examine the differences, we find that they have been caused, in the main, by prominent men's differing interpretations of Scripture, together with their failure to see another point of view. Because of the charisma of these men, others have followed them.

Separation for us today lies not just in being different from other denominations, but in our wholly realising our place in Christ and in our walking in accordance with that position. We are to acknowledge His headship and gather unto His name alone. We need to carry out His request to remember Him in the breaking of bread, to accept the Bible as the Word of God which contains the total revelation of God's purpose for mankind, and to wait for the moment when Christ calls His Church to meet Him in the air. With these before us, may we, in our day, get on with the repairs and once again enjoy the privilege and blessing of being separated unto Him!

5.
A mind to work

CHAPTER 4

SATAN'S WILES

This fourth chapter of Nehemiah has important lessons to teach us about our daily Christian life, with its conflicts, its difficulties, and, most importantly, the testimony we bear to Christ's Name. The chapter opens with another aspect of the enemy's attacks. So far, Nehemiah and the returned exiles had encountered a grieved enemy (2:10) and a mocking and scornful enemy (2:19). Now we come across a very indignant and furious enemy. There is a progression in the intensity of the enemy's attacks.

Satan does not change. God, in His mercy, has given us numerous examples in Scripture of Satan's workings and methods of attack. We need to take note of these lessons from Scripture to see how Satan organises the forces at his disposal to attack the believer today. So Paul warns us that we need to put on the whole armour of God to stand against the wiles of the devil (Ephesians 6:11). Paul warns the Galatian believers of the dangerous effects of leaven, that false teaching that Satan was seeking to promote among them. But Paul also encourages us that "the weapons of our warfare are not carnal but mighty in God for pulling down strongholds" (2 Corinthians 10:4). We can be thankful that not only are the warnings given us in Scripture, but we are also reminded of the resources available for our protection and comfort.

THE ENEMY GETS BUSY

The opposition is now united as they ready themselves to oppose the work of God. Having expressed their concerns to Nehemiah and the Jewish leaders about the plans for the rebuilding of the walls, Sanballat and his associates now turn to ridicule. Their hope was that the piles of rubbish and burnt stones would have been enough to dishearten the people. But this, like their earlier attack, was of no effect. Commenting on the history of the church, H. A. Ironside writes, "As the result of centuries of darkness and superstition, practically every precious truth of the Scriptures was overwhelmed by the ecclesiastical rubbish gradually accumulated". How we can thank God for the reformers of the 16th and of the 19th centuries!

Sanballat and company now decide on a frontal attack on their enemies. This must have been a fearful experience for Nehemiah and his people. Here was a fully armed force of men with all the weapons of siege against a partially repaired citadel defended by people who were not all from Jerusalem (see chapter 3). These people would have had concerns about their families, their homes, their livestock and their land. Today we are confronted by a Christian testimony that in many places is in ruins. Believers have concerns about domestic, family and business problems that, in many cases, seem to take priority over the call to serve the Lord. It is due to our neglect, unfaithfulness and failure that breaches and breakdown occur. The reminder from Proverbs 3:5-6 to trust in the Lord, acknowledge Him and He will take care of the outcome is something for all of us to remember and act upon. Paul, writing to the Colossians, insists on the pre-eminence of the Lord in our every day dealings (1:18).

Nehemiah must have realised that he was outnumbered and outflanked. From a human point of view, the job should be stopped and the workers sent home. There are times when we, too, looking around us at our churches, locally and nationally, become downcast by the failures, the lack of zeal, the lack of numbers. There is the temptation to give up the task and go home to our families, to business or to take up some leisure activity to fill our week. God forbid that these wayward thoughts become a reality!

TELLING GOD ABOUT IT

Nehemiah would have been able to cast his mind back to that day in the palace, to the night when he first surveyed the walls, and to the day when he announced his intention to the leaders of Jerusalem to rebuild. Similarly, it is good for us, at times, to look back over our lives and see the way the Lord has led us. So we can be reminded of past blessings which then encourage us for the future. Nehemiah turns to the One who, alone, had sustained, protected and encouraged him. He lays it all before Him with the words, "Hear, O our God…" (verse 4). He then identifies himself with the builders. He simply puts the facts before the Lord and gets on with the work! What an example for us today! If, instead of wringing our hands and talking about the problems that face us, we were to follow Nehemiah's example, we too would see blessing from God. If, like Nehemiah, we realised that the opposition is an affront to our God and we were in the good of this fact, we too would be more than conquerors through Him who loves us and died for us (Romans 8:37).

PRAYING AND WATCHING

The building progresses (verse 6) and provides two important lessons for us. Firstly, there was a unity of purpose amongst the people. They had a mind to work. Secondly, the opposition intensified. They became very angry and conspired to attack and cause confusion among the builders. We now come to an important moment in the rebuilding project. The builders' initial enthusiasm was starting to wane, their impatience was growing, and they were only at the halfway stage. Although they had had a mind to build (verse 6), now they are a little downcast: "There is so much rubbish that we are not able to build the wall" (verse 10). At this point, the opposition musters its troops. But we are told of the response of Nehemiah and the people: "We made our prayer to our God, and… we set a watch against them…" (verse 9).

Just to pray about the matter was, and is, not enough. There was a need to be watchful at all times, so they set a watch night and day. Paul reminds us that this attitude of praying and watching is necessary still today (Ephesians 6:18). There is a great need today to be diligent, to be aware of what is happening around us, and to be vigilant, so that the enemy is not able to infiltrate the church. Paul's epistle to the Galatians bears eloquent testimony to havoc carried out by the enemy within.

As we proceed down the chapter, there is another lesson. Jews and Samaritans were living side by side. Warning them ten times of the impending assault, and that there would be no escape for anyone, the Samaritans hoped that this would discourage the builders. What an effect this had when it was brought to the ears of Nehemiah! The people had laboured, prayed and watched. Now they have to prepare for conflict. They were to defend the wall (verse 13), their brethren, their families and their houses (verse 14).

GETTING PRIORITIES RIGHT

The order of these priorities is significant. The importance of the testimony of Jerusalem itself seems to be paramount, followed by the welfare of the brethren, then the family and, finally, the houses. Today, we seem to have reversed this order. Our homes seem to take priority, followed by family commitments, then the care of the brethren, and finally our Christian testimony. Time after time, we hear that family needs, house redecoration or repairs have top priority in our daily lives and the testimony has to take its place on the back seat. We ought to give more heed to our personal and corporate efforts regarding our Christian testimony.

Nehemiah organised the people to be able to continue the building work and put them in a strong defensive position, arming them so that they were ready should conflict arise. But most importantly, he encourages the people with the words, "Do not be afraid of them. Remember the Lord, great and awesome, and fight for your brethren, your sons, your daughters, your wives, and your houses" (verse 14).

DEALING WITH FEAR

It has been said that "Nothing is so much feared as fear". People of God throughout the ages have had to deal with this problem of fear. It is one of Satan's favourite methods to hinder the testimony of God and is used with great effect on most of us. Isaiah 12:2 gives us the recipe for overcoming fear: "Behold, God is my salvation, I will trust and not be afraid". Nehemiah's battle cry was "Remember the Lord" (verse 14). So Paul reminded Timothy, "Remember ... Jesus Christ" (2 Timothy 2:8), and counselled the Colossians that the Lord must have the pre-eminence in all things (Colossians 1:18). We need to heed these exhortations today. As we remember the Lord, we are reminded of His Person, His work, His worth, and also the place which He fills at the Father's right hand. With such a Saviour, Lord and Friend, why should we fear the enemy who has already been defeated at the cross of Calvary? Jacob was a man full of fear, who had had experience of God's goodness, who prayed but did not fully trust, and who finished up lame (see Genesis 32)! Let's take heed of the warning!

THE TROWEL AND THE SWORD

Our chapter now tells of the victory of this particular skirmish. Nehemiah does not say to the people, "Well, that's over, just carry on as before". He decides on a strategy that would help them to go on unhindered with the rebuilding of the wall. The company is divided into two parts, each part with a particular task. One company is fully armed for the defence of the city, the other carries on the building but still carrying a sword as well as a trowel (verses 16-18). These tools remind us of the word of God. The trowel aspect is used for the edification of the saints; the sword is used "to contend earnestly for the faith which was once for all delivered to the saints" (Jude 3).

But Nehemiah still has a further concern. The workers were scattered over the whole wall, and if the enemy attacked at a point where there were fewer people, there was the possibility of a breakthrough. Nehemiah uses a trumpet, an instrument with a strident sound. The trumpet had been used to assemble the camp of the Israelites in the wilderness, prior to moving on (see Numbers 10). It was also used to sound the alarm in case of attack. It was blown only by the priests, those men dedicated to the service of God. In Nehemiah's day, the trumpeter was one who "was beside me" (verse 18).

So the servant who sounds the message of the Lord today has to know the Lord's mind. He has to stand by Him; he has to experience daily communion with the Lord in order to deliver His message to His people. How we need servants today who are able to minister the word of God in this way! But there is equally a responsibility placed upon all of us to make sure that, by our presence at Bible readings, Fellowship Meetings, etc., we are in places where the word of God can be ministered under the direction of the Holy Spirit so that the oracles of God can be made known to His people.

In the closing verses of this chapter, we sense the devotion of the people. They laboured day and night in a two shift system (verse 21). Moreover, they all stayed near the job (verse 22). There were to be no deserters, no going home to see to things there. The key word was 'zealousness', and it was not confined to the labourers only. The rulers, the chiefs of families, the householders and their servants, together with Nehemiah, his brethren and his servants, all had this zeal. There is a deep need for a similar zeal to be evident in the assemblies today so that the breakdown in the testimony might be repaired.

SUMMARY

This chapter shows us how things can be done. In the Lord, we have the resources. But it is up to us to refuse to compromise with the spirit of our age. What a challenge this chapter brings before us! We need to question our zeal, our motives before the Lord, praying that we are not found wanting.

6.
Problems with the people
CHAPTER 5

Having dealt with the problems from outside the city, Nehemiah now has to face the strife within. As we look at this chapter, we see how much damage and, sad to say, animosity is caused by the enemy when strife between believers takes place. Many of us have experienced something of this during these past painful years. The Jews of Nehemiah's time were fully occupied with the dangers from without, but they had neglected their moral condition within. It is sometimes the case that those who are extremely zealous contenders for the truth, seeing so-called evil on every hand, have neglected the need for self-judgment in their own lives. To paraphrase James, "Where there is envy and strife, confusion and evil works follow" (3:16).

The apostle Paul was aware of this problem in the early church. He urges the Philippian believers to "let [their] conduct be worthy of the gospel of Christ" (Philippians 1:27). He wrote of the need to stand fast, to be of one mind, and to strive together for the faith of the Gospel. He warns the Galatians, "But if you bite and devour one another, beware lest you be consumed by one another!" (Galatians 5:15). How sad it is to witness groups of believers proclaiming the need from separation from evil-doers and what they judge to be false doctrine, but careless as to their own moral state!

The opening verses of this chapter find a parallel in Acts 6, where the problem was about the neglect of widows. Here we find the problem is between 'the haves' and 'the have nots'. Many of the people and their wives had exhausted their resources for every day living in their effort to rebuild the walls. Their Jewish brethren, by contrast, had plenty. The people had to eat to live but, in order to do so, were under serious obligations to their Jewish brethren. Children had been sold into slavery; houses and lands had been mortgaged – all with no prospect whatsoever of redemption. They were in absolute bondage, completely beholden to their Jewish brethren.

There is a danger in our day, particularly in the mission field where poverty abounds, when materially wealthy foreign nationals by so-called help cause the people there to be beholden to them. Needs of our poor brethren have to be met wherever possible, but without strings attached that make them beholden to their benefactors. Both in the past and still today this failure takes place.

To see the full effect of this serious problem, just have a look at Corinth. In the Corinthian church there were both rich and poor. Believers were even taking each other to court to establish their rights (see 1 Corinthians 6:1-11). We may not see this kind of behaviour in fellowships today, concerning temporal or material matters, but we do see the sad results of those who, wanting their own way, cause divisions.

Nehemiah, having seen and heard what was happening, now vents his feelings. He becomes very angry (verse 6). Here were a people who had experienced God's help and blessing, but were now placing their fellow brethren under a burden which was too much to bear. They had completely forgotten about God's instructions as to how they should treat one another when times became hard (see Leviticus 25:35-38). It is sad when those who work in the preaching of the Gospel start to impose burdens on new believers, so exchanging one set of burdens for another. When we were saved, the burden of our sins was removed. How sad it is when it is replaced by the burden of legalism!

How should this situation be corrected? As we read the following verses, we see how Nehemiah goes about this task. He does not immediately berate the leaders in his anger. He takes time to think things through. When problems occur, we tend to act impulsively. Of Nehemiah we read, "After serious thought, I rebuked the nobles and rulers" (verse 7). Those from whom he had once sought counsel (2:16-17) were the very ones he had to rebuke. In that time of serious thought, Nehemiah was totally alone but, being a man of prayer, he found his resources in God! Nehemiah's rebuke is not fudged; it is in the open, before the assembled people. Their wrong doing, exacting usury, which was not in keeping with God's instructions in Leviticus 25:36, was made known to all. So today in the church, the whole congregation has to be made aware of evil. In the past, there have been instances where wrong doings have been hushed up, either because of those who were involved or because it was thought by some to be too unseemly to bring to the light. Consequently these wrongs were never properly judged.

It is clear from what occurred in Nehemiah's day that every wrong act was made known. Nehemiah does not 'pull his punches' but neither does he continue to berate the guilty. He reminds them of their past acts and then presents their present obligation to their brethren. The guilty "were silenced and found nothing to say" (verse 8). What was classed as normal in a worldly sense – the taking of usury – had become acceptable within the testimony of God. In our day, we too should examine our dealings and relationships both with our brethren and with our work colleagues and neighbours to see just how much they are governed by what is classed as being acceptable in every day life in AD 2008! We, too, may well be silenced as we carefully examine our actions in the light of God's word. The people of Nehemiah's day had no excuse for their disobedience, and neither have we!

But God does not leave His people in limbo, as it were. Time after time in Scripture we find God acting in grace to restore His people. He is still the same today! The apostle John reminds us of what God has provided to restore our fellowship with the Lord and with His people (1 John 1:9; 2:1).

Nehemiah now says, "What you are doing is not good. Should you not walk in the fear of our God because of the reproach of the nations, our enemies?" (verse 9). Then he contrasts their conduct with his. He uses his conduct as a leader, or shepherd, amongst the flock of God as an example and guide to others. The apostle Paul behaved in just this way. He speaks about his lifestyle, working with his own hands in order to support himself (Acts 20:34-35). He could invite the Philippian believers to follow his example (Philippians 3:17). He reminds the Thessalonian believers of the kind of man he was amongst them (1 Thessalonians 1:5-6). Today, more then ever, we need men and women who walk in meekness and godly fear, not puffed up with knowledge, not desiring to lord it over others, but being living examples for the church.

Nehemiah was motivated by love and pity for the suffering of those around him. He was so grieved that the Lord was being dishonoured that he was ready to use his own resources to help the needs of others. What a lovely picture of Christ! Christ's attitude of humility and self-giving – "though He was rich, yet for [our] sakes He became poor, that [we] through His poverty might become rich" (2 Corinthians 8:9) – is seen in the actions of this man of God.

Nehemiah then appeals to the nobles and rulers to cease doing evil and learn to do well (Isaiah 1:17). As a result of their shame which he has exposed, he pleads with them to stop this usury. He expected results and the rulers confirm that they would restore what they had charged. Nehemiah, a man of great experience, does not simply take their word at face value. He calls the priests and requires an oath from them that they would fulfil their promise. He warns them of what God would do if they failed to keep their word, solemnly bringing the judgment of God before them. We can all, perhaps, readily identify occasions in our lives when, in the excitement of the moment, we say we will do something but, when we get home or in the cold reality of the next day, put it out of our minds. In Romans 14:10, Paul, writing about not too dissimilar circumstances, reminds us that we all have to answer for our words and deeds. The people of Nehemiah's day readily responded to his pleas, saying "Amen" and praising the Lord. In the light of our appearing at the Judgment Seat of Christ in a coming day, may we be equally ready to fulfil our word and carry out our promises!

PROBLEMS WITH THE PEOPLE

We are now given an account of Nehemiah's conduct as governor (verses 14-19). Looking at it from a human point of view, we might well feel that he is blowing his own trumpet. We have to remind ourselves that these actions are recorded for us in God's word and it is for our learning that they are there (Romans 15:4). Nehemiah had taken up the role of shepherd to the flock of Israel. The lesson for us is that the shepherds whom the Lord raises up for His people today should be examples to the flock (1 Peter 5:1-3).

As we look at these few verses, we see the generosity of Nehemiah. Rather than take from the people bread, wine and taxes, as he was entitled to do as governor, he provided for himself. He had identified himself with the people in the work of rebuilding the wall, not taking advantage of the poor and buying up land for himself. He made sure that all who were under his authority assisted in the work of rebuilding. In addition to all this, he was "hospitable" (1 Timothy 3:2). By his example, Nehemiah challenges us today. There is work for each one of us to do in rebuilding the testimony of God. We ought to esteem our brethren better than ourselves, not taking advantage of anyone (Philippians 2:3). We are to influence those of our households to assist in the testimony. We should give generously and be hospitable to others.

Nehemiah ends the chapter with a prayer: "Remember me, my God, for good, according to all that I have done for this people" (verse 19). He did not look for man's acclaim. Rather he desired God's commendation; he was looking for that "Well done, good and faithful servant" (Matthew 25:21). Nehemiah was a man who desired to do God's will and to glorify God in his everyday conduct. There is a danger, today, that ambition to get on at work, or in society, or in sport, takes all our energies. Nehemiah had his priorities right. He wanted to bring glory and honour to God and to be a blessing to the people of God. What are our priorities? The words of the hymn below challenge us to have the same desire as Nehemiah and to be here for the praise and glory of God (see 1 Thessalonians 1:6).

I have one deep, supreme desire - that I may be like Jesus.
To this I fervently aspire – that I may be like Jesus.
I want my heart His throne to be, so that the watching world may see His likeness shining forth in me – I want to be like Jesus!

Oh, perfect life of Christ, my Lord – I want to be like Jesus.
My recompense and my reward – that I may be like Jesus.
His Spirit fill my hungering soul; His power all my life control.
My deepest prayer, my highest goal – that I may be like Jesus!

7.
A personal attack

CHAPTER 6

THE SUBTLE ATTACK OF FRIENDSHIP

In this chapter, we come back to Nehemiah's personal history. The previous chapter was almost a parenthesis, where Nehemiah dealt with wrong doings amongst his own people. But now, in chapter 6, the old enemies of Israel re-appear. It may be that we do not read of these adversaries in chapter 5 because the people of God were doing their work for them! But now the method of attack has changed. It is no longer ridicule or outright opposition. Something far more subtle, friendship, is used to try to deflect Nehemiah from his God-given task.

It is good to see that Nehemiah is fully aware of the situation. The breaches in the wall have been repaired, but the doors in the gates had not yet been hung. Sadly, there are many in the church today who are unaware that there is still work to do. They turn up to one service a week, usually on a Sunday morning, but rarely at other times. Consequently, they are unaware of the needs of those in the church and of those tasks that need to be done.

Nehemiah was fully aware of the need to finish the walls. The testimony of God was of great importance; the need for separation from outside influences was of equal importance. Nehemiah had his priorities right. Consequently, he was not taken in when this message of so-called friendship came (verse 2). Nehemiah realised that this offer of friendship was false; its intention was to do him harm. This is surely a lesson for today that any overture of friendship from non-Christians needs to be examined with care. It may detract the believer from the task the Lord has given him to do. Nehemiah's reply to the invitation was masterful: "I am doing a great work, so that I cannot come down. Why should the work cease while I leave it and go down to you?" (verse 3). Are we as fully aware of the task in hand, of its importance and urgency in relation to the testimony of the Lord today? The hymn, "There's a work for Jesus none but you can do" challenges us as to the importance of the work before us, and the shortage of time in which to complete it. "Whatever you do, do it heartily, as to the Lord and not to men" (Colossians 3:23).

Nehemiah was marked by faithfulness. He had been given a commission and nothing was going to detract him from completing this task. Sanballat and his friends, the Samaritans, were marked by pretence: "They feared the LORD, yet served their own gods" (2 Kings 17:33). Like some in Christendom today, they were professors only, pretending to owe allegiance to the Lord but not serving Him.

The enemy is not deterred by this first refusal. Four times they sent this same invitation and four times they received the same answer! The same tactic is still used today – invite them often enough and they may be shamed into accepting! This method was used very successfully by

A PERSONAL ATTACK

Delilah on Samson (see Judges 16), and caused his downfall and death. Let us remember Nehemiah's successful method of dealing with this kind of attack. The answer is, "Sorry. I have work to do."

LIES AND CRITICISM

Having failed with their conciliatory approach, the enemy changes tactic. Still pretending to be friendly, they attack Nehemiah in an open letter detailing three things that had supposedly come to their ears. To verify these reports, Sanballat names his source. The reports suggested rebellion against the authorities, usurpation by Nehemiah, and the appointment of prophets to proclaim a new king in Jerusalem. This letter insinuated that all Nehemiah's work was unauthorised, that Nehemiah himself was position seeking, and that he was embracing religion to further his aims. The enemy, not really knowing Nehemiah, uses lies in his attempt to stop the work. So the Lord rightly describes the devil, "...there is no truth in him...he is a liar and the father of it" (John 8:44). A similar attack was made by Tertullus against Paul, accusing Paul of being "a creator of dissension among all the Jews throughout the world, and a ringleader of the sect of the Nazarenes" (Acts 24:5).

We do not have to look very far in our day to see similar tactics still being used. Sanballat's remedy was, in effect, "Come on. Let's talk it over. Let's be reasonable about this rebuilding business." Compromise is a political tool and one used by Satan on a regular basis. It has no place in the witness and testimony of the church, particularly where the truth of God is concerned. Nehemiah's answer was blunt and to the point (verse 8). In that same spirit, we might say today, "Your imagination is running away with you. All you want to do is to stop or dilute the testimony".

Sadly, we see around us, in this once Christian Britain, the effects of compromise. In the name of pluralism, the church is expected to be politically correct! For the sake of the testimony, we have to be on our guard and, like Nehemiah, realise what is being attempted. Nehemiah knew the resources that were available to him. This man of prayer soon made his request known to God (verse 9). It was direct and to the point. There was no flowery language, just the words, "O God, strengthen my hands".

THE ENEMY WITHIN

In verse 10, Nehemiah comes face to face with yet another problem. This time it is from one of the Jews, resident in Jerusalem, one who would benefit from the protection that the wall afforded. Shemaiah does not, however, appear to have been involved in its building – "he was shut up" (verse 10, AV), probably unwell. (But note NKJV translation, "a secret informer".) Here was a man purporting to be a prophet, seemingly hospitable towards Nehemiah. His name (meaning 'heard of Jehovah') and his pedigree gave the impression of his being a faithful follower of the Lord. In reality, he was a traitor!

Sadly, there are those in the church today who have knowledge and ability but, for some reason or other, shut themselves up. Then they are open to all sorts of attacks from the devil, rather than assisting in the testimony of the church.

Shemaiah's advice to Nehemiah was that they should go and hide because Nehemiah's life was in danger. He did not suggest that they leave Jerusalem but that they should hide in the temple. But in the temple, Nehemiah would be hidden from the view of the people who depended on him for leadership. By right, the temple was a place for the Levites. Had Nehemiah followed this advice, he would have dishonoured the Sanctuary and would have been guilty of desertion from his God-given task. Those engaged in the building would have been disheartened and the building would have ceased. Sanballat would have achieved his end! The testimony, as seen in an unfinished wall, would have been derisory.

However, Nehemiah realised that the prophecy was not from God. Likewise, we today have the God-given ability to know what is of God and what is not. "But you have an anointing from the Holy One, and you know all things" (1 John 2:20). John continues to expand on this gift from 1 John 3:24 through to 1 John 4:6. He reminds us that "He who is in you is greater than he who is in the world" (1 John 4:4)!

Nehemiah's bold declaration, "Should such a man as I flee?" is the hallmark of the overcomer. Nehemiah knew that he had the authority to carry out the task of rebuilding the walls and he had experienced the good hand of God upon him. We, too, should live in the reality of our faith. "And this is the victory that has overcome the world – our faith" (1 John 5:4). Nehemiah came to realise that the company of the prophets, the same group who had helped in the rebuilding of the temple in the days of Ezra, were also on the payroll of Sanballat and Tobiah. Moreover, there was amongst them a prophetess, Noadiah, whose name means 'Jehovah assembles'. How sad it is when there are those who gather with the Lord's people today but who, through their contact with the world, seek to bring its influences on assembly life, to the detriment of the testimony!

Nehemiah, having seen through the plan, takes the matter to the Lord (verse 14) and leaves it there. The hymn encourages us to "take our burden to the Lord and leave it there", while Peter reminds us, "Casting all your care upon Him, for He cares for you" (1 Peter 5:7). Our problem is that we are too independent. We try to solve our own problems, with all the attendant unnecessary burdens, sorrows and cares that this brings when we fail to take them to the Lord in prayer.

THE WORK IS FINISHED!

Verse 15 is a tremendous understatement! While Nehemiah had been under attack from his enemies, the work had not stopped. It was finished in just fifty two days! Their enemies could not but hear of it, and the nations around saw the completed walls (verse 16). When God works amongst His people, the work is seen and is the subject of general conversation in the neighbourhood. The work of the Lord can not be hidden! So the Lord promised that whatever the opposition against His Church, "the gates of Hades shall not prevail against it" (Matthew 16:18). His Church will be victorious!

We should take heart as we remind ourselves of what took place in Nehemiah's day. Today, there are attacks upon the church from many sources – secularists, agnostics, atheists and those who advocate political correctness. Sadly, their influence is being felt in the church. The enemy today is no different from that in Nehemiah's day. Those who are leaders in the church need to make a stand against those who oppose the truth and others who want to water down the truths of Scripture. In Nehemiah's day, the prime source of opposition came from Tobiah. Because of family relationships, his good deeds were brought to Nehemiah's attention. We need to guard against unhelpful family influences in the church today.

The walls of Jerusalem would speak to us of a number of aspects of the Christian life. They remind us of security,

A PERSONAL ATTACK

separation and testimony. Security for the believer is to be found primarily in Christ, but also in the fellowship of other believers. Scripture reminds us of this important aspect of fellowship (Hebrews 10:24-25). It is in this fellowship that we can care for one another and so show to the world our love for one another as we carry out the Lord's commandment (John 13:34-35). Those walls now physically separated Jerusalem and its inhabitants from those without but, sadly, the inhabitants were still very much under the influence of those outside. There is a parallel in the church today where there are those who appear to walk a path of separation from the world, but whose private and home lives are no different from the world around them. As a result, the testimony is marred; the reputation of the church is harmed and its influence no longer felt. The enemy has been successful! We very much need today, like the first Christians, to continue, "steadfastly in the apostles' doctrine and fellowship, in the breaking of bread, and in prayers" (Acts 2:42).

In the next chapter we will see what Nehemiah did to remedy the deficiencies amongst the people of God.

8.
Restoration

CHAPTER 7

Although the chapter, from verse 6, is largely taken up with genealogy, there are some important lessons for today that can be learned from the first five verses. They deal with the restoration of the life of the city and with the order for daily worship in the temple. They also highlight those individuals who had proved faithful throughout the difficulties experienced during the rebuilding of the walls. It is not intended to deal with the genealogy which is almost a repetition of Ezra chapter 2*. It should be noted that verses 70-72 provide a more detailed list of gifts to the work. In order to maintain the testimony in Jerusalem, order had to be restored (verse 1). It will be instructive to look at the details of this.

THE GATEKEEPERS

In appointing gatekeepers (or porters), Nehemiah showed that he was aware of the need to maintain vigilance regarding what was happening outside the city. In this

---

* See *Lessons from Ezra* by the author, published by Scripture Truth Publications, 2007, ISBN: 978-0-901860-75-0

way, he would ensure that no evil would have access into the place where God's name was honoured. Today we, too, have a responsibility to be vigilant as to the encroaching influence of this present evil world (Galatians 1:4). On every hand, we see the effects of this influence.

Fashion is one area which can exert its influence on many of us. Paul, writing to Timothy, emphasises the need for modesty in apparel (1 Timothy 2:9). It appears that in today's fashion, it is not what is worn but what is exposed that counts! There is a temptation to older as well as younger to follow this trend. Are our gatekeepers failing in their duty, for fear of offending some, in drawing attention to this trend? The gatekeepers in Nehemiah's day had the task to shut the gates, not only on the Sabbath, but whenever it was necessary. From what we read, this caused uproar both in as well as outside the gates (see Nehemiah 13). We may not appoint gatekeepers in the church today, but their tasks ought to be maintained. Older sisters in the church in Crete were to instruct the younger ones (Titus 2:3-5). Today there is a need for this practice to be continued.

In Christendom in general, the task of the gatekeeper has almost disappeared. Church councils meet, it seems, to find ways of accommodating the trends practised by the world – and woe betide those who object! The gatekeepers were first allocated their duties by King David (1 Chronicles 26:1-19). They were men of pedigree, from the tribe of Levi, whose fathers had carried the ark, the Tabernacle and its furnishings through the wilderness. They were people who valued and cared for the things of God. We need to question ourselves as to the value we place upon the things concerning our Lord Jesus Christ. What is our appreciation of His person, His work and His word?

The Singers

As well as the gatekeepers, singers were appointed (verse 1). The singers were first installed by King David for Solomon's temple (see 1 Chronicles 25). They were from three families, some 288 in all, and were divided into groups of twelve. In Nehemiah 12, we read of two choirs, drawn from villages around Jerusalem, who sang at the dedication of the walls. The thought of the singers would suggest to us today those of God's redeemed people who willingly offer the sacrifice of praise to the Lord (Hebrews 13:15). In Nehemiah's day, they sang so that the joy of Jerusalem was heard a great way off. While our singing must, in the first instance, be offered to the Lord, it would be good if our singing was as attractive to those who heard it. One of the problems of singing together can be that each has his or her own idea as to how fast, or slow, the tempo should be. We do not listen to the others with whom we are singing or, in some cases, to the accompanying instrument. Consequently, the song of praise becomes almost a discordant sound.

The Levites

The Levites are also mentioned (verse 1). These were the people whose task it was to assist the priest in the daily services of the temple. They had the mundane tasks of making sure that there was water in the laver, that there was enough wood for the brazen altar, that the ingredients for the incense were in the storehouse, as well as numerous other tasks needed for the offering of the daily sacrifices. Without their help, the temple worship would be the poorer.

From 1 Timothy 3:8-13, it would seem that the corresponding tasks in the church today are to be carried out by the deacons. We do not have the laver as in Tabernacle and temple days, but there is still a need for the cleansing and the refreshment of God's word to be made available. We need to be reminded of what took place on the altar of Calvary, and we need that supply of spiritual incense to help us to offer that sacrifice of praise unto God.

In addition, there are the more mundane tasks which still have to be done in each assembly. These include the cleaning, the setting out of the chairs, the heating arrangements, the disposal of gifts and the paying of bills. All these need to be undertaken by someone. Sadly, it is often left to one, with little help from others. When Paul wrote to Timothy, the task of the deacon was not a solitary one. There were several deacons in a local church and, in today's situations, there is still the need for such. Are we helping to fulfil these tasks or are we just turning up expecting everything to be in place?

Hanani and Hananiah

In verse 2, we see that Nehemiah gives his brother, Hanani, and Hananiah, the ruler of the palace (or 'commander of the citadel'), charge over Jerusalem. Here were two dependable men. "He was a faithful man and feared God more than many" may refer primarily to Hanani. It was Hanani who had first travelled from Jerusalem to Shushan to share with Nehemiah the desperate need in Jerusalem (1:2). It is good to see that, amongst all the problems and difficulties, here was a man who was consistent. Here was a man at the hub of things; he was aware of the difficulties and problems of the day and was willing to do something about them. There is a need today for men of God who are aware of matters as they may arise to take the lead, but not lord over, each assembly of God's people.

Hanani was marked by his faithfulness. There are still those who, thank God, are still among us and who carry on the task given to them no matter what the difficulties in which they may find themselves. These men and women, on whom many fellowhips are dependent, keep things going week by week, come what may. Faithful to what they have been taught and believe, they would teach others those same truths (2 Timothy 2:2). What a need there is for such today in the church worldwide!

The other feature that marked Hanani was that he was God-fearing. This is not being terrified of God, but rather giving to God the reverence due to Him as Creator, Redeemer, Saviour; recognising Him as the One who is immortal, dwelling in light unapproachable (1 Timothy 6:16), yet the One whom we are privileged to know as our Father. Hanani knew God only as the Almighty. He had seen with his own eyes how God had preserved and restored the remnant of Israel. He would have heard from Ezra how God's good hand had been upon them as they had journeyed back from Babylon. Hanani would have seen the rebuilding of the temple, and would have heard from Nehemiah how God had answered his prayer for his people. He would have seen how God had enabled those few people to rebuild the walls of Jerusalem and would himself have experienced the blessing of God. Today, we also can look back upon our lives and see how the Lord has been working. We can see how blessing has been showered upon us. We recognise thankfully that we have been brought into the good of God's purposes, brought into the knowledge of His secret, the mystery of the Church (Ephesians 3:2-6).

The work to be done

Having given the credentials of the men who had the responsibility for the groups mentioned in verse 1, Nehemiah now details the duties they were to discharge. In particular, they were to oversee the gatekeepers – that group of men who were responsible to uphold the safety and integrity of Jerusalem. The gates had to remain closed until the sun was up (verse 3). In other words, they had to be able to recognise who were coming through the gates. No enemy was to be admitted. In our day, when visitors arrive for the breaking of bread and are not known to us, it is necessary to ascertain who they are and from where they come. Usually they would bring a letter of commendation with them to verify who they are and, in turn, to bring the greetings of their local assembly (2 Corinthians 3:1, Romans 16:1).

But we see in verse 3 that the gatekeepers were to be vigilant not only at their watch station, but also at their own front doors. This surely is another salutary lesson for us. Sadly, in our day, there are things which may not be seen in our fellowships, but have gained access into our homes. We see how Satan has gained access through materialism, television soaps, family ties and a host of other things. To obtain the things which we have been led to believe are necessities for every day living, we are working longer hours to pay for them, no longer able to support midweek meetings and even cutting back on our time spent in the presence of the Lord. The need to earn more in order to buy more has taken a pre-eminent place in our lives, excluding the One who is pre-eminent by right (Colossians 1:18).

As in Nehemiah's day, today there is a shortage of people to fulfil the tasks for the smooth running of the assembly.

Many places have to rely on the faithful few to be there, to oversee the week by week functioning of the assembly. Help is needed! God put it into Nehemiah's heart to gather the nobles and the people together so that they might register by their genealogy (verse 5). He was to question their right to be there in the land. We cannot carry out such a task because only the Lord knows those who are His (2 Timothy 2:19). But the Lord has also said, "By their fruits you will know them" (Matthew 7:20). We should be able to discern how believers are progressing by their walk and by the effect they have on others (1 Timothy 4:15). In Nehemiah's day, there were those who had to be excluded from the people of God (verses 61-64). They were not able to establish the fact that they truly belonged to Israel. Today, in the church at large, there are those who do not produce evidence of their new birth and their new life in Christ. May we each one give evidence in our lives in our assembly, at work and at home, that we love the Lord, that we faithfully follow Him, and diligently serve Him according to His ways!

9.
Renewal

CHAPTER 8:1-12

THE FEAST OF TRUMPETS

Jerusalem was now secure; the inhabitants were fully accounted for. The people were all in their respective cities (7:73). Chapter 8 opens with a general sense of security. But there was still another issue to be met. It was the seventh month, the month of the three feasts of the LORD (see Leviticus 23). On this, the first day of the month (verse 2), the Feast of Trumpets was to be held. This feast was instituted to remind the Israelites that throughout their wilderness journey, it was God who had directed their way. He had instructed Moses to make two silver trumpets (see Numbers 10:2). The blast of one trumpet was to summon the leaders; the sound of both trumpets was the signal for the people to begin their journey. During the Feast of Trumpets, the people would reflect upon all the way in which God had led them.

As we look for a lesson for us today, it might be suggested that the sound of one trumpet has already taken place. Israel is back in the Land, albeit in unbelief; the leaders have been assembled. As Christians, we await the sound of the trump of God, summoning us to meet the Lord in the air (see 1 Thessalonians 4:16-17). In the meanwhile, it is good for us, too, to have a time of reflection and remind ourselves of what God has done for us during our lives. As the hymn writer reminds us, "Count your blessings, name them one by one, and it will surprise you what the Lord hath done". Such reflection should surely cause a note of praise to rise from our hearts.

This chapter, and Ezra 3, open with the same words: "...the people gathered together as one man..." It is good when people have a sense of well-being, are happy with their lot and are aware of their obligations to the Lord. But we need to beware of any sense of self-satisfaction! One thing was missing here, and the chapter begins by identifying what it was. There was the need for the people to be aware of God's requirements so that they might walk in obedience to His will. So the book of the law of Moses is brought out; the people go back to basics.

AWAKENING TO GOD'S WORD

Today, we, too, need to be governed by the word of God. Throughout the Church's history, all awakenings and revivals have been brought about by the revealed word of God, the Bible. In Old Testament times, Josiah was given the book of the law found in the temple (2 Chronicles 34). Hezekiah also had an awakening based on the revealed word of God (2 Chronicles 30). John Wycliffe (1320-1384) was a forerunner of the 16th century Reformation when men like Martin Luther (1483-1546), William Tyndale (1490-1536) and John Calvin (1509-1564) were awakened to re-introduce truths that had been lost in the Dark Ages. All these men sought to bring the people back to the word of God. In the 19th century, God used men like J.N.Darby and his associates to revive truths of God that were no longer being presented to the Church.

These men searched the Scriptures, seeking the truth that was contained in them, in order to live according to it. Sadly, in the Church today, the truths that those men found and lived by are no longer treasured and, in some cases, are even being rejected and put to one side. Just as failure marked the Jews in the days of Josiah and Hezekiah, so it has marked all the revivals during the Church's history. However, the resources that were available to the men of history are available to us in our day. The word of God stands unchanged. It is unerring, abiding and readily available to all in many parts of the world.

As we look into the chapter, a number of salient points catch our attention. The first is that, in gathering in Jerusalem, the people had responded to the call of the trumpet. It is only those who have first responded to the call of the Gospel who are able then to respond to the truths contained in Scripture. The people gathered, as one man, in the open square that was before the Water Gate (verse 3), the place which reminds us of the refreshing, cleansing and reviving abilities of the word of God (Ephesians 5:26). The people were all of one mind. "Behold, how good and how pleasant it is for brethren to dwell together in unity" (Psalm 133:1). Having arrived at Jerusalem, the people could now experience the joy of fellowship with one another.

BRING THE BOOK

It must have been a wonderful sight for Nehemiah as he looked out of his house to see the crowds of people. What a thrill as he saw that the city was now secure and the safety of the people was established! The walls with their gates were functioning properly; the gatekeepers were in position and all seemed well. There must have been a sense of thankfulness to God for the way in which He had been their help over the past months during the rebuilding of the walls. What the visiting people thought we are not told but they were like minded.

We can identify with this feeling today. How good it is to gather together with the Lord's people. Such occasions ought to be times of real joy. How sad it is when meetings for fellowship are arranged but some do not take advantage of the opportunity to meet with fellow believers! The people in Nehemiah's day gathered together with real joy and with a great desire to know more about the things of God as revealed in His word. Ezra was told to bring the book of the law of Moses (verse 1). What a cry went from their lips: "Bring the Book!"

Is this Book, the Bible, our first call, or do we just read what others have written on it to obtain our teaching? The people might have had a testimony meeting, as it were. They might have listened to Nehemiah giving an account of the rebuilding of the walls, or to Haggai relating how he and Zechariah had encouraged the people to complete the rebuilding of the temple, or to Zerubbabel's account of the re-introduction of temple worship. No doubt they would have been encouraged by all this. But no! The cry goes up, "Bring the Book!" The people wanted to know for themselves what the word of God had to teach them in their day.

It should be the same for us today. Let our desire be to know what God wants to teach us. We have God's written word, the Bible, and the illumination of God's Holy Spirit, the One whom the Lord Jesus promised would "guide [us] into all truth" (John 16:13). What others have written on the word of God can be helpful and we should not ignore the gifts God has given to His church in this way. But we need to beware of giving them more credence than Scripture itself. The need to go back to the Book is as great today as it has ever been!

Praise to God

Having brought the book, Ezra reads from it (verse 3). This is the first time in this book of Nehemiah that Ezra is mentioned. Scripture records its own testimony to this faithful servant of God: "This Ezra went up from Babylon; and he was a ready scribe in the law of Moses…Ezra had prepared his heart to seek the law of the LORD, and to do it, and to teach in Israel statutes and judgments" (Ezra 7:6, 10, AV). Ezra might be described as 'a platform man', a man able to fill the pulpit. Often in the past, and sadly also in our day, the pulpit has been occupied by men who are not fully equipped to do so. Ezra was a man who not only knew the book, he had experienced the "good hand of his God upon him" (Ezra 7:9) in his journey up from Babylon and had expressed his thanks for it.

Now in verse 6 of our chapter, Ezra blesses "the LORD, the great God". What a moment this was! The people were affected by Ezra's thanksgiving and echoed their 'Amen's, worshipping the Lord with due reverence. How encouraging it is to hear all the Christian company join in saying 'Amen' when prayer and thanksgiving is offered! This can be particularly encouraging to those who may be somewhat hesitant in taking part publicly.

Teaching God's Word

Ezra had become aware of a problem – the people who gathered that day in the square in front of the Water Gate were a people to whom the Hebrew spoken language was almost foreign. During, and after, the captivity, Aramaic had become the language of everyday use. To overcome the problem, Ezra summoned more helpers. There were thirteen of them (verse 7), besides those who occupied the steps of the pulpit (verse 4). Between them, "they read in the book in the law of God distinctly, and gave the sense, and caused them to understand the reading" (verse 8, AV). What a responsibility those men had! But the responsibility today is no less for those who occupy the platform to minister God's word! How important it is to read the word of God distinctly. How sad it is if listeners have difficulty in following the public reading of the Bible. It is sometimes read much too fast, without due care and reverence. The pronunciation of some of the names of places and people shows a lack of research. There are numerous aids available for the proper pronunciation of biblical names. It behoves those who occupy the pulpit to have such a publication to hand so that they, too, are able to read distinctly.

Not only did they read distinctly, they gave sense to the reading of the word (verse 8). Ezra was well acquainted with the Scriptures and was able to instruct others (see Ezra 7:6). The fact that Ezra was able to have helpers alongside him at the public reading is evidence of his diligence in teaching the word. If there is a lack of teachers today, it is not God's fault. The gifts are still available to the church, through the Spirit. It is our fault if they are not used.

Timothy was instructed to pass on what he had learned from Paul to faithful men who would be able to teach others also (2 Timothy 2:2). We have God's treasury of truth at our disposal. We are responsible not only to display it in our day, but also to ensure that those who follow are fully aware of its value. Those who occupy the pulpit must make sure that their hearers understand what is being said. We now live in the 21st century, an age of rapid communication. We need to become acquainted with, and be able to use these methods to pass on our spiritual heritage.

LIVING AND POWERFUL

In verse 9, we see the amazing power of the word of God: "All the people wept when they heard the words of the law". Hebrews 4:12 reminds us, "For the word of God is living and powerful, and sharper than any two-edged sword, piercing even to the division of soul and spirit, and of joints and marrow, and is a discerner of the thoughts and intents of the heart." Verse 9 is a demonstration of this living, powerful word of God. Further consideration of verse 9 brings before us yet another aspect of the word of God. Nehemiah, Ezra and the Levites use it to bring comfort and refreshment to the people.

The people gathered at the Water Gate had had a severe shock as they listened to the reading of the book of the law. Their consciences had had a rude awakening; they deeply felt their guilt, and that of their fathers, in refusing to obey the word of God and were grief stricken. It is only when man is at the end of his tether that God can move in to help. What words of comfort are expressed by those in the pulpit: "This day is holy to the LORD your God; do not mourn nor weep." What a day! We, too, can look back to a day, or time, in our lives when we believed the word of God that "Christ died for the ungodly" (Romans 5:6). That was a day holy to the Lord, our second birthday and a happy day for us!

The joy of the Lord

What an exhortation now proceeds from Nehemiah, culminating with those wonderful words, "The joy of the Lord is your strength" (verse 10). The people were told to appreciate what they had and to share it with others. In Jerusalem at that time there were some people who had nothing. They, too, were to be brought into this same joy.

In this affluent, material age, there still exists a great spiritual need. A few years ago, there was a song in the 'Hit Parade' entitled "(I can't get no) satisfaction". Little did the song-writer realise just how true those words are for, without Christ, there is no lasting joy. As a hymn writer has put it,

> *I tried the broken cisterns, Lord,*
> *But oh, the waters failed!*
> *E'en as I stooped to drink they fled*
> *And mocked me as I wailed.*

Thank God there is an answer and the same writer knew it. So the chorus reads,

> *Now none but Christ can satisfy,*
> *None other name for me;*
> *There's love, and life, and lasting joy,*
> *Lord Jesus, found in Thee.*

Let us in our day rejoice in the God of our salvation, becoming more acquainted with His word and so appreciating its contents in a much deeper way. This will lead us to enjoy the extent of the blessing into which we have been brought. In this way, we will be moved to bless the Lord our God and to share the blessing with those who have nothing.

10.
Obedience and Refreshing
CHAPTER 8:13-18

ASKING FOR MORE

"Bring the Book!" What a request! It was what those returnee Jews asked for who on the feast day of the seventh month assembled "as one man" in the open square before the Water Gate (Nehemiah 8:1). When Ezra started to read "the book", they answered, "Amen! Amen!" as with hands uplifted but faces towards the ground they worshipped the Lord (verse 6). From early morning to mid-day they stood listening to the reading of the Word. As H. A. Ironside noted, it had six different effects on them that day, namely, uniting; desiring; solemnizing; reverencing; refreshing; and, finally, obeying. And as they heard the Levites explaining the sense of the Word, their sorrow was turned to joy: "The joy of the LORD is your strength" (verse 10).

Then they asked for more of the same on day two (verse 13)! Reading produced in the people a deep desire to understand the words of the Law. Is our desire to please the Lord who has saved, redeemed, and reconciled us to

God? Well, in order to carry out this desire, we too have to be aware of what is, and what is not, pleasing to the Lord. We become aware of these requirements by reading, understanding, and obeying His Word. Reading and intellectual understanding are readily embraced by many Christians today. But, sadly, *obedience* to the Word is often overlooked. It seems that, as long as we are happy in our fellowship, or assembly life, it doesn't matter whether we are fully obedient to God's Word or not. How often do we hear the phrase, "but we have found happy fellowship!" from someone who has departed for "pastures new", where the truths that they once held dear are not fully adhered to. The whole object of the reading of God's Word, on that first day of the seventh month, was that it would result in obedience.

We too, in our day, must realise that the Word of God is not only the Word in which we find the way of salvation, but also the Word of our instruction, and a manual for our lives as Christians. "For whatever things were written before were written for our learning, that we through the patience and comfort of the Scriptures might have hope" (Romans 15:4). In the letters to the seven churches, the Lord writes to the church at Philadelphia, "I know your works. See, I have set before you an open door, and no one can shut it; for you have a little strength, have kept My word, and have not denied My name" (Revelation 3:8). Obedience to His Word was what won His commendation. Too often we read the Bible like a novel or history book, something we can take or leave as it suits us. Little do we realise the *power* it has within it. "For the word of God is living and powerful, and sharper than any two-edged sword, piercing even to the division of soul and spirit, and of joints and marrow, and is a discerner of the thoughts and intents of the heart" (Hebrews 4:12). Sadly, some neglect serious reading and understanding the Word, and the benefits of this. James has words about this neglect. "For if anyone is a hearer of the word and not a doer, he is like a man observing his natural face in a mirror; for he observes himself, goes away, and immediately forgets what kind of man he was" (James 1:23-24). In other words, the Word of God hasn't had an effect on that person's life. The challenge to us today is, are we affected by the Word of God as it is read and ministered? Too often, we feast on "roast preachers": we appraise their style, presentation, and delivery, but do not digest what has been made available for our instruction and encouragement from the Word of God!

OBEDIENCE AT THE FEAST

There was a period of 13 days between verses 15 and 16 of Nehemiah 8 (compare Leviticus 23:34). During this period the proclamation went out to all Jerusalem and to the cities and villages round about, that on the fifteenth day of the month the celebration of the feast would take place. No doubt some in those places had not attended the Bible reading and were startled by the proclamation, and had to be persuaded to keep the feast. Similarly, there are those today who rarely attend the reading or ministry meetings, and consequently do not fully appreciate why we gather in simplicity to the Lord's Name. There is a need to renew the proclamation, reaffirm the truths believed and announce plainly why we meet in the way we do, and what the basis is for this stand. Many in Christendom, mistakenly, think it is because we like a meditative approach to worship, that we hold a Breaking of Bread on Lord's Day morning, without priests, an announced order of service, or any musical accompaniment. They do not fully realise the basis of our gathering.

As a result of the proclamation the Feast of Tabernacles was celebrated in the prescribed manner for the first time since the days of Joshua (see Numbers 29:12-39). The returnees from Babylon had previously celebrated the feast (Ezra 3:4), but not in the prescribed manner. Often we are also guilty of celebrating the feast in a way that is unfitting for the occasion. We lack the preparedness, and the time for quiet meditation before the meeting. We come in at the last minute, or late.

The people did not come empty-handed. Receiving instructions to bring branches of olive, palm and myrtle trees and make booths (Nehemiah 8:15), this they did. These three trees, we are told, differ in their heights when full grown, and in what they bear.*

The palm tree grows to about twelve metres (40 ft) and produces dates. This signifies effort in order to produce the sweet fruit. The olive tree is not so tall, about five metres (16-17 ft), but it has to be regularly pruned to keep the head compact. It is a long-lived tree whose primary purpose is to produce oil, though the fruit can also be eaten as it is. The fruit is harvested by beating the tree, then the olives are pressed for oil: this, again, speaks to us of effort. Finally, the myrtle is a bush about two metres high (6-7 ft), producing fragrant flowers in summer. In this tree we find something that attracts and is for display. As we ponder these three trees, they suggest a lesson for ourselves. We, too, have to gather together something to bring with us, when we come together to meet with the Lord's people. So often we come empty-handed when we meet around the Lord's table, and have nothing for the Lord, so that the meeting suffers. The remedy for this is the effort that the palm and olive tree symbolize: only

---

* See *Bible Plants, Fruits & Products* by Tom H. Ratcliffe, published by Christian Year Publications, 2002, ISBN: 978-1-872734-26-2

through effort do we enjoy the sweetness of the things of Christ. This is the constant task that we have to undertake in order not to quench the Spirit. We also have to keep our eyes fixed on the Lord in His glory and beauty – the myrtle tree. It is then, and only then, that we can prove and enjoy the promise that Paul makes when writing to the Corinthians, "Eye has not seen, nor ear heard, Nor have entered into the heart of man The things which God has prepared for those who love Him" (1 Corinthians 2:9).

> *Oh, fix our earnest gaze*
> *So wholly, Lord, on Thee,*
> *That, with Thy beauty occupied,*
> *We elsewhere none may see.*

"Then the people went out and brought them and made themselves booths" (Nehemiah 8:16). They were obedient to the instructions, and made space for the obedience of others. The booths were erected on housetops, courtyards and in the open squares of the Water Gate and the Gate of Ephraim. The housetops suggest the people of Jerusalem attending to their own obedience in this matter, the courtyards, perhaps their relatives or friends, and the open squares those from a distance. But all of the booths were built within the confines of Jerusalem. Being within the walls offered the blessings of safety and security to any visitors. And as the mere sight of Jerusalem brought a sense of relief to the traveller (Psalm 125:1-2), how much more would that sense be enhanced by tabernacling within the walls! Analogously to the days of Nehemiah, we realize in our day that in Christ, Mount Zion, we too have safety and security, and this enables us to express the joy that our salvation brings. The Feast of Tabernacles was a joyful time: a time to remember how God had redeemed, cared for, fed, and preserved the nation: "And there was very great gladness" (verse 17). Surely, as we recall redemption's story, and realise what we have been brought into, having been forgiven, reconciled, justified, and sanctified to God, and as we think about the One who has brought it all about, we should rejoice with similar "joy inexpressible and full of glory" (1 Peter 1:8).

A WHOLE WEEK OF THE BIBLE

They kept the feast for the prescribed seven days (Nehemiah 8:18). For seven days the Word was read; for seven days they listened intently. These "seven days" look forward to the day of the Kingdom, when the Prince of Peace will have revealed Himself in all His glory, and have set up His Kingdom. His authority having been established, the nation of Israel will be at peace and there will be gladness in the land, as Israel obeys the Word of the Lord. For our present lesson, the emphasis of verse 18 should be placed on the Word being read each day. In the earlier celebration of the feast of Tabernacles immediately after the original return from Babylon (Ezra 3:4), the emphasis had been on the sacrifices. We might ask, why the change in emphasis? The answer surely is that in times of revival different truths are brought to the fore. Unlike Ezra 3:4, Nehemiah 8 has occupied us with the importance of God's Word. The lesson for us today, as we are privileged to handle the word of God, concerns how we treat it, heed it and obey it. The Jews of Nehemiah's day can certainly teach us that lesson. They *honoured* the word: they stood up when it was opened (verse 5). They *listened* when it was read, and desired to understand it when it was expounded (verses 2-3; 7-8; 12-13). They *rejoiced* when they understood it (verse 12), and, finally, they *obeyed* it (verse 17). Sadly, we live in a day when the Word is denied, watered down and in some cases ignored. When this is the case, there is no testimony, no harmony, no security, and no joy. The important lesson for us is to become re-acquainted with the Word; to honour it, for it is where God has revealed His purposes; to heed it, for it is our guide; to listen to it, for it is the source of knowledge; to obey it, for it is our source of joy.

AND AN EIGHTH DAY

And on the eighth day there was a sacred assembly – a new beginning, a new day (verse 18). This speaks of an eternal day that is yet to come, when the new heavens and new earth will have been established, Satan having been cast into the lake of fire (Revelation chapters 20-21). It will be the day when tears, sorrow, and death will have been done away, when the words recorded for us in Revelation 21:1-5 will have been fulfilled, when the marriage of the Lamb will have come, and the Church will have been displayed as the bride adorned for her Husband. Then God will be all and in all. All this is future, but we see the start of it on the glorious resurrection day. The commencement of the eighth day for us was when Christ was raised from the dead. This was the day that the victory was won. His words to the disciples that day were, "Peace be with you" (John 20:19), and, thank God, those words are still the same today for every believer. Three times in that chapter of John's Gospel the Lord granted his disciples peace. We can enjoy that peace today – in part. "And the peace of God, which surpasses all understanding, will guard your hearts and minds through Christ Jesus" (Philippians 4:7). The hymn writer, knowing something of the peace and love of God that is found in our Lord Jesus Christ, wrote:

> *Father! Thine own unbounded love*
> *Has reached us through Thy Son;*
> *We now behold Him crowned above,*
> *Eternity's begun.*

As we continue to testify for our faith in the day in which we live, and whilst we look on to that day of wondrous promise, let us, like the people of Nehemiah's day, respect, reverence, heed, and obey God's Word.

11.
Repentant prayer

CHAPTER 9

REPENTANCE AND SEPARATION

What effect should Bible-reading have?

Confession, separation, more Bible-reading, and prayer leading to action! The eighth chapter of Nehemiah records the main activity during the first Feast of Tabernacles of Nehemiah's governorship of the province of Judah. The – rather sparse – numbers of Jews who had returned from exile all eventually came together to celebrate it (8:2, 17) – that was impressive. What was more impressive was that they demanded that the Word of God be read to them, on the first day, the second and all the other days of the Feast (8:1, 13, 18). Genuine revival begins with a hunger for the Word of God. Do we see that today, in a time when Bible and Scripture-reading societies are reporting a decline in Bible reading? These Jews made their "convention" truly a "Bible convention"!

It is easy to be affected emotionally by what is taking place in large conventions of Christian people. The disturbing reports of the so-called "Toronto Blessing" of the mid-

1990s are a regrettable instance of this. It is also possible for those who address large numbers of people to use what could be termed "the cosy chat" method to warm people up in their "comfort zones", by telling them about God's wonderful love, without addressing the hard question of sin and the need for repentance.

The attenders of the Feast in Nehemiah 8 also were deeply affected by their eight-days' experience. So affected indeed, that they were still there on a ninth day, after the prescribed feast-days had ended. But *how* were they affected? Fasting, sackcloth, and dust on their heads (9:1)! Personal repentance was the effect of hearing the word of God. The Law had reached their consciences, affected their lives, and caused this change in their appearance and demeanour. This demonstrates the true effect of the living Word of God on someone who bows to its authority. All too often, however, we ignore the Word when it is read and explained, due to what we give priority to in our lives. This causes weakness in our witness, lack of interest in attending Christian meetings and little or no blessing in the Gospel.

The second effect of their eight-days' Bible reading broaches an unfashionable topic. "Then those of Israelite lineage separated themselves from all foreigners; and they stood and confessed their sins and the iniquities of their fathers" (9:2). The word "Israelite" marks them out as God's chosen ones (compare Amos 3:2). Today, those who truly belong to the church of God are the chosen of God in Christ (Ephesians 1:4). Like these repentant Jews, they have been affected by the word of God, repented of their sins, and separated themselves from the things of the world as they confessed their need of God's mercy and grace. The Israelites of Nehemiah's day didn't stop at half-measures: they "separated themselves from all foreigners".

Though the truth of separation has an important positive side to it, this emphazises the negative side. The Christian requirement today is not to separate physically from unbelievers (1 Corinthians 5:10; though compare 1 Corinthians 10:14; 2 Timothy 2:22). But the New Testament is full of warnings about the character of the world and the need for moral separation from it.

We are exhorted, "Do not love the world or the things in the world. If anyone loves the world, the love of the Father is not in him" (1 John 2:15). John repeatedly writes of our relationships with and to the world. He warns us about its false prophets, its transience, and its opposition to the Father (1 John 2:16-23; 4:1). But he also encourages us about our victory over it: "For whatever is born of God overcomes the world. And this is the victory that has overcome the world – our faith" (1 John 5:4). When we remind ourselves of what is in the world, as John characterizes it, it is amazing that we continue to embrace some of its facets and enslave ourselves to its trends. There is a tendency today to pick and choose the things which we exclude from our daily lives according to the world's current standards, rather than God's standards. We have come to tolerate practices that are commonplace in today's world, with the consequence that the world has affected the church and continues to. Sometimes we make the excuse that we are only doing what has been done before. There is a need to confess our sins as well as the sins of those who have gone before. James, too, uses very strong language about friendship with the world: "Adulterers and adulteresses! Do you not know that friendship with the world is enmity with God? Whoever therefore wants to be a friend of the world makes himself an enemy of God" (James 4:4). Separation from the world is a very serious subject: studying the word of God makes us realise how important it is in the eyes of a holy God. May we all fully realise the immensity and importance of this truth, confessing our sins and failures before Him.

MORE OF THE BIBLE

Having separated themselves from all foreigners, they then "stood up in their place and read from the Book" (Nehemiah 9:3). That is, they occupied the ground of truth that they had been brought into – so should we – and they desired to learn still more of what Scripture reveals – so should we. Sadly, we find amongst some younger people the tendency to find a place of fellowship that suits them and gives them a sense of well-being, the yardstick of the Scriptures being seldom applied to the situation. This is not what took place in Jerusalem in Nehemiah's day. Neither is it what has taken place in the revival-history of the church through the ages. There is no blessing without personal cost. The people, it is said (verse 3), stood for a quarter of the day to hear the word of God; and for another quarter of the day, they confessed and worshipped the Lord their God.

How important it is to confess the Lord both individually and collectively! It is as we confess and own Him as Lord that we experience some measure of His greatness and grace. Realising His greatness in obtaining our salvation at Calvary, and the immensity of His grace in meeting our needs leads our hearts to worship Him. These people in Jerusalem knew about deliverance, safety and security. They had been delivered from Babylon, and had managed, against all odds, to rebuild the walls of Jerusalem, which, together with the gatekeepers posted, gave them a sense of safety and security. Having seen the Lord's hand with them, it is little wonder that they stood confessing and worshipping the Lord their God. The basis and the cause of worship today is reflecting on what the Lord has done, on what He continues to do day by day, and on the prospect of being with Him in the place of safety and security that He has gone to prepare for those that love Him.

The catchy tunes, repetitive phrases and noisy bands with so-called "worship leaders", that have become prevalent in many evangelical circles, are not what lead our hearts to worship "in spirit and in truth", but, rather, a deep sense of the greatness, goodness and grace of the Lord and our privilege of being in the presence of One so holy. This is worship. We share the same deep emotions that Thomas experienced in the upper room when the Lord said to him, "Reach hither thy finger" (John 20:27-28, AV).

A GREAT PRAYER MEETING

This reading of the Law had a remarkable effect on some Levites (Nehemiah 9:4). It caused them to identify themselves very prominently in front of the people that had gathered in Jerusalem. They did not hide their light under a bushel (Luke 11:33), but stood on "the stairs of the Levites". This was one of the places of access into the Temple Court. It may have been the place from which, in former times, the Psalms of Ascent (120-134), had been sung as the people entered the temple. Thus these Levites took a place where they couldn't be missed and from that place led the people in a prayer that also exhorted, encouraged and reminded them of things which the Lord their God had done for them. This act, which took place so long ago, is repeated in many different ways today. Faithful servants of God often remind us of His greatness, grace, mercy and love bestowed upon us throughout our lives. It is recorded that Mattaniah led the thanksgiving psalms, he and his brethren (Nehemiah 12:8). The meaning of his name is worth noting: 'God is Primeval' or, 'God First, self last'! What a place of privilege this man had as he led the people in thanksgiving! And as we gather each Lord's Day to remember the Lord, this privilege is granted to the brother who gives out the first hymn, thus leading the thanksgiving. It also behoves us to remember that the first hymn usually sets the theme of praise for the meeting, and it should be one that draws our attention to the Lord.

These Levites' prayer is probably the longest prayer recorded in the Scriptures. In it there are many lessons for us today. Its opening phrases centre on the greatness of God and on the place where He dwells. It has a ring of what is generally called, "The Lord's Prayer".

Verse 5 reminds us of the *supremacy* of God, and how important it is to praise His glorious Name at all times. Verse 6 brings forth the *Creator* God. Whilst even in our atheistic day many accept that there is a Creator God, it is only the believer who has accepted Christ as Saviour who acknowledges that "all things were made by him; and without him was not any thing made that was made" (John 1:3, AV). This truth is reiterated in Colossians 1:16 and Hebrews 1:2.

Verses 7-8 show us the *sovereignty* of God, in the way that He called Abram from Ur, and gave him a new name and an inheritance. This surely reminds us of God's sovereign work in our lives. Paul, writing to the Ephesians, brings to the readers this tremendous truth that we, too, are called by God, and have been given an inheritance (Ephesians 1:4, 11). The apostle Peter described that inheritance as "incorruptible and undefiled and... reserved in heaven for you, who are kept by the power of God...." (1 Peter 1:4-5).

Verses 9-11 of the prayer turn to the *redeeming* work of God. The Levites recount how God, the Redeemer of Israel, had delivered them from the bondage of Egypt. They recite how God had seen the affliction of their fathers, heard their cry by the Red Sea, and worked wonders against Pharaoh, dividing the waters of the sea so that the people passed through on dry land. Surely the remembrance of this mighty work, as well as of what God had recently accomplished, would enlarge the listeners' sense of the greatness of their God and increase their gratitude towards Him. As we reflect on the infinitely higher cost of our redemption – the precious blood of Christ – we, too, should have that sense of awe, wonder, and gratitude and be filled with praise.

Verses 12-15 recall the *grace* of God, in the way that He cared for the people; guided them with the cloud and the pillar; gave them the Law, so that they could live orderly lives before Him and with one another; and, for their physical needs, instituted the Sabbath and gave them manna and water. God, who had brought them out of Egypt, now brought them through their wilderness journey.

GRACE AND COMMITMENT

But, as the behaviour of the Israelites on that journey is recollected in verse 17, we see God as a *forgiving* God. The verse summarises "the ways of God in grace", calling to mind the lines, "Who is a pardoning God like Thee? Or who has grace so rich and free?" In spite of all their waywardness, God brought them into the land. We can rest assured that God's purposes are never thwarted. But we also see how in spite of all the blessings of redemption through the blood of Christ, according to the riches of God's grace, and of the very faith to believe (Ephesians

1:7; 2:8), we fail in our Christian pathway, and have to be chastened. This is a mark of sonship. "For whom the LORD loves he chastens, And scourges every son whom he receives" (Hebrews 12:6). The prayer before us also relates the wonderful moment when God brought them into the land. The victories of the way had been accomplished, the Canaanites had been subdued and it was the time of the harvest (Nehemiah 9:22-25).

Then the prayer comes to the sad and sorry tale of Israel's disobedience in the land. It states that "they cast your law behind their backs" (9:26): how sad it is that today in Christendom we see many disregarding the Word of God, and also belittling those who faithfully uphold the authority of the Scriptures. Perhaps it is because of the general departure from the Word of God that we, in Western Europe, are witnessing a decline in moral standards, often led by governments passing laws that promote what is abhorrent to God.

But in this prayer we also see, that at the times when the people fully realised their helplessness and turned to the Lord for help, He heard their cry and gave them deliverers (9:27). Correspondingly, in the church's history, there have been men of God who have brought about a restoration in its testimony after failure. Men, such as Huss, Calvin, Luther, the Wesleys and Whitefield, Darby, Kelly, Spurgeon, Moody and latterly Graham, were used by God to bring deliverance, salvation and restoration. The influence of these men of God has sadly waned and, once again, we see the effects of the work of Satan in the church and in society. Verse 28 states "Therefore You left them in the hand of their enemies". This dreadful situation rather resembles what is around us today. The enemy of our souls seems to be in control. However, we take courage as we remind ourselves that "whom the LORD loves he chastens, and scourges every son whom he receives" (Hebrews 12:6). The Lord assures us of His love even when times are dark, and we experience, like Israel, that God is indeed gracious and merciful (Nehemiah 9:31).

As the Levites on the steps led the people in this prayer, they came to a point where the only thing left was to confess their failure and the sin of the people. Thankfully, they didn't leave it at that. They took the next step of making a covenant to renew their allegiance to the Lord (9:32-38). In this last part of the prayer they acknowledge God's greatness, faithfulness and goodness, and cast themselves on His mercy. In our day, the day of grace, it is good for us, as individuals as well as collectively, to be reminded of the way that God has worked in our lives. Stocktaking is an important annual task in every business. It also should be regularly undertaken in our spiritual lives. It is only then, when looking back over our lives, that we shall see the way God has worked in them. When writing the hymn, "Rise my soul thy God directs thee"*, Darby appears to have looked at the way God had been involved in his pathway, and thus penned the moving words: "What the God that thou hast found." We, like the Israelites of old who were prepared to write a sure covenant (9:38), should renew our efforts to serve the Lord, more fervently and faithfully, whilst we wait for His return. For as the last verse of the hymn referred to reminds us:

> *There no stranger-God shall meet thee—*
> *Stranger thou in courts above—*
> *He, who to His rest shall greet thee,*
> *Greets thee with a well-known love.*

---

* No. 76 in *Psalms and Hymns and Spiritual Songs, Selected 1978*, published by Scripture Truth Publications, 1989, ISBN: 978-0-901860-39-2; from the poem "God in the Wilderness" (1837) in "Spiritual Songs" by J N Darby

12.
A new beginning

CHAPTERS 10 & 11

PEOPLE FOR GOD

Nehemiah 10 describes a re-dedication – not of walls (this didn't come until 12:27-43) – but of *people*. Nehemiah 11 describes a freewill offering of *people*.

Hard work (chapters 3-7), hearing God's word (chapter 8), and repentance and prayer (chapter 9) roughly describe the sequence of events in Nehemiah up to the start of chapter 10. By the beginning of chapter 10, the people's consciences had been awakened by the good hand of God upon them in the rebuilding of the walls and the re-establishing of order in city and temple. Re-acquainting themselves with God's word, they had repented, and heard the Levites' prayer, reminding them of what God had done for them throughout their history. That prayer had ended with an undertaking to make a covenant of re-dedication to God. The first twenty-seven verses of chapter 10 list the names of those who "sealed the document". These comprised the governor, twenty-two priests, seventeen Levites, and forty-four leaders of the people.

A NEW BEGINNING

What a picture of a nation, small though it was, whose government, religious leaders and heads of families all vowed to walk in faith before the Lord! What a contrast to our day, when those in government have disregarded any "form of godliness", embraced secularism and all that goes with it, promoted homosexuality, and legislated against the conscience of those who wish to be governed by Scripture. Even some so-called leaders in the churches disregard the teaching of Scripture and condone evil practice.

True, the scene depicted in this chapter was a very poor second to the glorious conditions and assemblies of the days of David and Solomon. This was only "a measure of revival in our bondage" (Ezra 9:8). Small and weak, at best, and under the domination of a world power, nevertheless this remnant, because of their repentance regarding their nation's sins and their total reliance on God, were wonderfully blest. This should encourage us. God does not restore that which once flourished to its pristine glory; but, instead of bemoaning "the day of small things" (Zechariah 4:10), we should in faith accept the situation we find ourselves in, repent and re-dedicate ourselves: this is the way of blessing. In a day of breakdown, when men are no longer prepared to accept the authority of Scripture regarding relationships between male and female, and many follow them, we need to examine ourselves and follow Nehemiah's compatriots' steps of re-dedication. They realised the value of God's word and acted upon it, even at the cost, subsequently, of bitter sorrow and humiliation. This needs to be done today.

Those leaders who placed their seals on the covenant of re-dedication were then joined by the rest of the people in placing themselves under its terms (Nehemiah 10:29).

Though drawn from all walks of life, they all did this with knowledge and understanding of the implications. There were no "free-riders". To live a life for Christ in this present world needs similar action. There is the need for knowledge of the Scriptures, an understanding of them, and a life of dedication to live by them. But, unlike the people of Nehemiah's day, born-again believers of our day are indwelt by the Holy Spirit who enables them to live a life which is pleasurable to God. Verse 29 also indicates the value of *fellowship* and its power to strengthen commitment to the requirements of this re-dedication: they "joined with their brethren".

COMPREHENSIVE RE-DEDICATION

Their covenant of re-dedication had five definite clauses:

1) To walk in God's law.
2) To maintain separation from the peoples of the land.
3) To observe the Sabbath and to let the land lie fallow.
4) To deal graciously with their brethren.
5) To do what was needed to maintain the regular temple service.

Brought into New-Testament terms, these five clauses present a great code for Christian living:

1) God's Word must have its rightful place of authority in our lives day by day.
2) We must walk a path of separation – from the world, but to the Lord, avoiding being "unequally yoked ... with unbelievers" (2 Corinthians 6:14).
3) We should set aside the Lord's day as a special day; and recognise our responsibility for the good things God has committed to us.

4) We should care for our fellow believers.

5) We should recognize our regular responsibility in the maintenance of the testimony of God.

This is a very comprehensive covenant; it covered every part of the lives of the returned exiles, and every day of the week too. Its first clause, indeed, committed them to obedience to the Word of God *in its entirety* (verse 29). And our dedication to the Lord and His Word must be similarly comprehensive. Do we "cherry pick" – do we accept the Scriptures that suit our lifestyle and wilfully ignore the rest? Too often we compartmentalise our lives. We place mental barriers between our family life, work life, leisure life, sport life, church life (sad to say, often in that order). And our "dedication" only reaches some of these compartments. Is that dedication at all? It is questionable whether those who live like this have any positive input to the life, fellowship and testimony of their local church. When Paul wrote his instruction to the young church in Colossae, he stressed the position that the Lord has in relation to every aspect of the believer's life (Colossians 1:18).

RE-DEDICATION IN DETAIL

The second clause of this covenant indicates a twofold responsibility – for ourselves, and also for our families (Nehemiah 10:30). Designed to ensure that no foreign influence entered the family, its counterpart for us is given by Paul in 2 Corinthians 6:14-18. Are we, as parents and even grandparents, making sure that the influence of the world is not entering our households? Sad to say, there is a lot of failure on this score. Its effects are evident in the behaviour, dress mode and demeanour of many families in the church today. It often shows itself in a lack of reverence at formal worship gatherings – in casual attitudes and disrespectful clothing. We meet with our Lord, the most wonderful Being in our lives and what do we do? Before and immediately after the meeting there is chatter about what took place during the week, how the football team fared and many other mundane things. It is sad to say that, in some cases, our dress sense does not befit the occasion. Should we be invited to meet the Queen or some other dignitary, we would dress for the occasion; yet we, His purchased possession, allow the casualness that marks the age in which we live to colour our dress, behaviour and demeanour. As gathering to the Lord's Name, and claiming His presence in the midst, we ought to sense His greatness and the glory of His person in a spirit of reverence and awe, and feel the privilege of being in His presence. When the priests entered the temple, they took off their everyday garments and put on the priestly garments befitting the place and the service of the Lord GOD (compare Ezekiel 44:17-19).

The third clause of their covenant had three parts. Firstly, it bound them to respect the Sabbath Day by not trading during it. We know that we do not belong to that past dispensation, and that we are not under law but under grace (Romans 6:14). But the undertaking of these Jews has a lesson for us. Do we allow greed for material gain, family commitments, holiday travel and other tasks to come before the request of the Lord to remember Him? Sadly, there are some believers who practise attending once a week, *so that* the things of everyday life can otherwise carry on undisturbed. In His wisdom God gave the instruction to the Jews to "remember the Sabbath day, to keep it holy" (Exodus 20:8). The principle of keeping one day of the week different from the remainder is well worth carrying out. To give just a day – one out of seven – to be occupied with the Lord's Person, work and worth has given spiritual as well as physical refreshment to the church since Pentecost. The first lines of poetry that Frances Ridley Havergal wrote were:

> *I gave My life for thee,*
> *My precious blood I shed,*
> *That thou might'st ransomed be*
> *And quickened from the dead;*
> *I gave My life for thee,*
> *What hast thou given for Me?*

To this they annexed a vow to "forgo the seventh year's produce" (compare Exodus 23:10-12). This challenges our faith. It represented a great step of faith for these Jews, with all the uncertainty of the enemies around them. As we look to the uncertain future of our fellowships, what part does our faith play? Do we rely on human ability and material wealth to keep the testimony in our area going, or do we totally rely on the Lord? Sometimes "living by faith" is viewed as a sort of special calling for some of God's servants. Here the whole congregation signed up to this undertaking and in this, the church's day, all believers are called upon to live by faith and not by sight (2 Corinthians 5:7). We tend to think that if everything is in order to our satisfaction, this does duty for dependence on the Lord. We may check that we are gathering on what has been termed "divine ground", and that our gatherings are outwardly and ecclesiastically correct, sometimes putting up false barriers of reception to achieve this; yet lose our hold on the eternal realities.

The final part of this third clause - sufficiently important to be listed separately - pledged them to cancel debts every seventh year (Nehemiah 10:31; compare Deuteronomy 15:2). Do we sometimes exact hard and self-righteous demands of one another, alienating those whom we ought to have drawn with cords of love, and causing unnecessary distress to our fellow believers? Concerning the famished crowds whom the disciples wished to send away, the Lord said, "You give them something to eat" (Matthew 14:16). It is our responsibility to care for and feed the flock of God, and pay heed to the Lord's command not to send them away. We can see the chaos in the assembly that has been caused by division and schism, due to the exaction of harsh demands by some on their fellow believers. Our Lord's "new commandment" (John 13:34-35) has flown out of the door and self righteousness has entered; demands for apology have been required instead of acts of reconciliation. Looking back, we must all say (even the best of us) that we are a poor witness. As the "day of grace" draws to a close, and, sadly, the word of God is being given up in parts of the church, surely those who seek to cling to the Word should cease exactions of another. Rather, all alike judging everything that has hindered fellowship, we should put away the evil things that have wrought havoc, and stand together in fellowship with each other, and in testimony to the world that we belong to the Lord.

By the final clause of their covenant the people of Nehemiah's day undertook to do what was needed to maintain the regular worship in the temple. This also involved the whole congregation – priests, Levites and the people. Some had the task of collecting wood for the burnt offerings; others of attending to the ordinances respecting first-fruits. Whatever the task, it was to be done willingly. It was only with regard to money that an obligation was placed on the whole community. They were to pay an annual tax of one-third of a shekel "for the service of the house of our God" (Nehemiah 10:32-33). A silver shekel, weighing 0.364 troy oz, is, at today's value of sil-

A NEW BEGINNING

ver, approximately £5.00. The requirements for the service of the house of God did not demand great sums of money but a small offering was required. In the time of Christ the temple tax was the equivalent of two days' wages (compare Matthew 17:27). Today there are many needs in connection with the service of God: running expenses of buildings, maintenance of His servants at home and abroad; support of literature – the list is endless. We are not under any obligation as to how much we give to the work of the Lord, but the Scriptures remind us, "So let each one give as he purposes in his heart, not grudgingly or of necessity; for God loves a cheerful giver" (2 Corinthians 9:7). If the people of God are right individually, then what is corporate will flourish, and there will be abundant provision to maintain a visible testimony. Lack of spirituality closes up hearts and wallets; whereas godliness opens both. May we, like the people of Nehemiah's day, be determined not to neglect this.

A HUMAN FREEWILL OFFERING

Chapter 11 appears to consist mainly of a list of names, whose meanings shall not be more closely studied in this instance. But verses 1-2 contain a further lesson. They detail another free will offering, not of possessions, but of men willing to serve God in Jerusalem. The city defences needed to be maintained and manned, the temple had to function as the place of worship, good government had to be done. To fulfil these tasks, people had to live in Jerusalem. The leaders of the people resided there; but for the rest of its population, lots were cast so that ten percent of the returned exiles occupied the city. Yet those on whom lots fell were described as volunteers whom the rest of the people blessed! It is sad when the majority in a fellowship give no thought to the few "volunteers" on whom the burden of building maintenance falls. The volunteers for "Jerusalem service" came from every section of society. There were ordinary tribesmen (verses 4-9), priests (verses 10-14), Levites (verses 15-18), and Nethinim who resided in Ophel, a part of Jerusalem almost adjacent to the temple (verse 21). They didn't have far to travel to get to their place of service for the Lord! Let us, in our day, by the grace of God, follow the example of these volunteers in our walk, worship, praise and testimony, and occupy a place where Christ is rightfully exalted at the centre of the gathering.

13.
A dedication parade
CHAPTER 12

MEN OF GOD REMEMBERED

Chapter 12 is divided into three parts. Verses 1 to 26 list names of the priests and Levites who came up to Jerusalem with Zerubbabel and Joshua following the decree of Cyrus (Ezra 1:1), and their descendants. Verses 27 to 43 describe the dedication of the walls of Jerusalem. Finally 12: 44 – 13:3 indicate (i) the responsibilities of those who were assigned to the upkeep of the temple worship, (ii) the responsibilities of the whole people for the support of such persons, and (iii) the need for the people to be separate from the surrounding nations.

Verses 1-7 list by name twenty-two priests who returned, and not just by family as in 7:39. Half of these names include the name of Jehovah. The first name, Seraiah, means 'Jehovah is Prince'. The last name, Jedaiah, means 'Jehovah is Praise'. The other names denote characteristics with which we would do well to identify. The name Ezra, meaning 'help', surely suggests a needed characteristic in the society in which we live. Another interesting name is

Iddo. Meaning 'opportune', he was possibly the father / grandfather of Zechariah the prophet, whom the Lord used along with Haggai to encourage the people during the rebuilding of the temple (12:16; compare Zechariah 1:1).

Then, in verses 8-9, Levites' names are listed. Since two of them coincide with the names of Levites who were said in 11:17 to have volunteered for "Jerusalem service", it could be that this list, unlike that of the priests in 12:1-7, is not historical but pertaining to Nehemiah's own time. The Levites "led the thanksgiving [psalms]" (verse 8). What a privilege in our day to be able to set the theme of worship, simply by giving out the first hymn; and what a responsibility also, to perform this task faithfully! These lists teach us that God in His grace takes notice of all tasks done for Him. No matter how trivial we may think them, He records them. Small tasks, carried out faithfully week by week by people who do not seek the chief place in the church, are important. Someone ensures that the doors are open in time; someone else that the room is clean and tidy. How poorly we appreciate these apparently little tasks done so faithfully, if we complain about the heating system being too hot or too cold, or the footstools being in the wrong place!

Verses 10-11 give a list of five generations of the line of high priests from Jeshua to Jaddua; and history records a Jadduah who was a great and celebrated high priest in the days of Alexander the Great – about 110 years after Nehemiah's time. This little paragraph may have been added at a later date, as also verse 22, if "Darius the Persian" is Darius Codomanus, the Persian monarch overthrown by Alexander. It is possible that these additions were done in the time of Malachi. Or maybe these identifications are incorrect. But the resolution of this puzzle is not our concern. "Holy men of God spoke as they were moved by the Holy Spirit" (2 Peter 1:21), and all that they wrote is "for our learning" (Romans 15:4). And our Lord said "The Scripture cannot be broken" (John 10:35).

The integrity of the temple was maintained by the gatekeepers (verses 25-26). The temple of Nehemiah's day was poor in comparison to Solomon's, and yet the insignificant remnant who had custody of it sought to act on divine instructions communicated by David to Solomon at the beginning. We, likewise, no matter how feeble and weak our testimony, must go back to that which was from the beginning and endeavour to carry out what is written in God's word.

DEDICATING THE WALLS

The second section of the chapter runs from verse 27 to verse 43, and describes the dedication of the completed walls of Jerusalem. Nehemiah must have felt great relief and joy at seeing the crowds of rejoicing people arriving in Jerusalem for this great day. It was a day for people and leaders to reflect on how God had blessed the small band that had accompanied Zerubbabel and Joshua back to the uninhabited ruin of Jerusalem, how He had encouraged those first returnees into rebuilding the temple and deflected the opposition of those opposed to it. Then they would also reflect on their personal experience of the good hand of God in the dangerous rebuilding of the walls that they had participated in. As the crowds around the walls viewed the completed structure with excitement, wonder and awe, they wanted to praise God who had done such great things for them (12:43).

In the time of the millennium the walls of Jerusalem will be called "salvation" and its gates "praise" (Isaiah 60:18). How often do we reflect on and rejoice in our salvation and lift up our voices in praise? Do we share with our fellow believers what the Lord has done, and what He is doing in our lives, and so give them, with ourselves, cause for joy and praise? If the walls of Jerusalem gave a sense of safety, and to enter into that place of security brought forth praise and thanksgiving in the day recorded for us in this chapter, we too should have a similar thrill as we reflect on the great salvation that has been wrought by the Saviour for us. We often ask our brethren to pray for us in times of trouble, but mutual rejoicing in what the Lord does for us, in this apparent day of weakness, is equally needed. Too often we stare only at the blemishes of those we meet with, and fail to focus on the greatness of what the Lord has accomplished on our behalf.

Verse 30 tells us that "the priests and the Levites purified themselves, ... the people, the gates and the wall." Everything and everybody was included in that act of purification. "The lesson this has for us is obvious. We may state it in a few words – No dedication without purification" (F. B. Hole). There has to be a spiritual purification of our lives in order that we may take our place as worshippers. David learned about the need for personal purification, and wrote of it in Psalms 51:2 and 119:9. Isaiah clearly states the same (1:16). In Romans 12:1 Paul emphasized the need for practical holy living, and in 2 Corinthians 7:1 for clean living. Thus, what was the responsibility of the priests and Levites in Nehemiah's day is the responsibility of every believer today. Thankfully we have been cleansed by the precious blood of Christ (1 John 1:7), and Isaiah 1:18 shows the dramatic change brought about by that cleansing power. But there also has to be that daily cleansing by the application of the word of God described in Ephesians 5:26 ("that He might sanctify and cleanse it with the washing of water by the

A DEDICATION PARADE

word", AV); and, in exhorting us to "draw near with a true heart in full assurance of faith", Hebrews 10:22 adds "having our hearts sprinkled from an evil conscience and our bodies washed with pure water." When this has taken place in our lives, and only then, we can offer the "reasonable service" of Romans 12:1.

Nehemiah gathers the princes and leaders of Israel on the wall and forms two companies to lead the praise (Nehemiah 12:31-43). What a scene of triumph! What a testimony there was to the surrounding peoples in the successful rebuilding and repairing of the walls and gates through the help of God, in spite of the enmity of Sanballat, Tobiah and Geshem, of adverse conditions and of the poor materials available! Never should we lose sight of the greatness, resources and power of our God (Ephesians 3:20-21). It is only through our lack of faith that we fail to avail ourselves of them.

These two companies formed two choirs, one led by Ezra and the other by Nehemiah, which ascended the walls, one going to the right and the other to the left, and both arriving together at the house of God, the temple – the place of praise and worship. We can almost visualise the scene, the two choirs singing as they marched, the two groups, priests and Levites, answering one another in the manner of Psalms 24:7-10 and 136. Well might they fill the courts of the temple with the chorus, "Oh give thanks to the Lord for He is good! For His mercy endures forever." The song of praise was raised, and worship, in the form of "great sacrifices", was offered throughout the day on the brazen altar in the midst of the Temple Court (verse 43). What do these sacrifices teach us? It is not enough if we just stop at the singing and the excitement this sometimes generates: what about the worship? Is there that sense of awe, and an appreciation in our hearts of the Lamb of God? Do His perfections thrill us as we think of who He is, what He has done and the wonder of the salvation that He accomplished for us at Calvary? Do we realise how much God the Father appreciates the Son and the work He has done? Do we realise the privilege that is ours in experiencing the nearness of being in the presence of the Saviour? It is when this occurs that worship from our redeemed hearts flows out to God. The hymn writer summed up the sense of worshipping hearts:

> *Gathered to Thy name, Lord Jesus,*
> *Losing sight of all but Thee,*
> *Oh, what joy Thy presence gives us,*
> *Calling up our hearts to Thee!*
>
> *Blood-bought, reconciled, forgiven,*
> *Here Thy death we love to show,*
> *Waiting till above in heaven,*
> *All Thy glory we shall know.*
>
> *Oh, the joy, the wondrous singing*
> *When we see Thee as Thou art,*
> *Thy blest name, Lord Jesus, bringing*
> *Sweetest music to God's heart!*
>
> *Notes of gladness, songs unceasing,*
> *Hymns of everlasting praise,*
> *Psalms of glory, joy increasing,*
> *Through God's endless day of days!*

"DOING GOOD AND COMMUNICATING"

The remainder of the chapter (verses 44-47) describes how the people of that day arranged the upkeep and maintenance of the daily services in the temple. They also were concerned about the support of the priests, Levites, singers, and gatekeepers who kept the charge of their God by carrying out the tasks prescribed for the functioning of

A DEDICATION PARADE

the daily temple worship. The people made sure that there were provisions, and clean storehouses to receive the tithes, thus fulfilling the requirements of the Law of the LORD in giving portions for the priests and the Levites (see Numbers 18:8-32). We also have an obligation to meet the needs of those among us who seek to serve the Lord. Although Paul wrote that he knew how to be abased, our responsibility is to ensure that, wherever possible, the Lord's servants are provided for.

The writer of the letter to the Hebrews reminds us of the twofold offering that we are to make: "Therefore by Him let us continually offer the sacrifice of praise to God, that is, the fruit of our lips, giving thanks to His name. But do not forget to do good and to share, for with such sacrifices God is well pleased" (Hebrews 13:15-16). These two offerings should not be separated – thanksgiving going up to God from grateful hearts, and generosity towards men and fellow believers in particular. This is the practical expression of our gratitude to God. We live in the day of the welfare state. The government appears to have taken out of our hands the opportunity to help the poor but if we look around there are still many ways of alleviating hardship. For instance, giving advice to those who need help in a strange land: we live in a land where there are many immigrants and, sadly, in some places, the church is unaware of their needs. Nehemiah's people honoured God with the first-fruits of their substance, and we should do so too. We are reminded by Paul that God loves a cheerful giver (2 Corinthians 9:7). Malachi 3:10-12 clearly tells of what God expects from His people, and what God does in return. We are stewards not only in spiritual matters but in material ones too. We are happy to sing the first lines of Frances Ridley Havergal's hymn,

> *"Take my life, and let it be*
> *Consecrated, Lord to Thee;*
> *Take my moments and my days,*
> *Let them flow in ceaseless praise,"*

but often have problems with the lines that ask,

> *"Take my silver and my gold,*
> *Not a mite would I withhold…"*

Let us always remember that all that we have has been given to us by the Lord and that we owe our all to the One who is the "Giver of all good".

It appears that what is described in chapter 13:1-3 took place the same day. These verses introduce the subject of separation, which is expanded in the remainder of the chapter. For now, it is sufficient to say that separation is the practical outcome of cleansing. As chapter 13 is dealt with, practical examples of failure, as well as the exhortation to be vigilant, will be brought to the attention of the reader.

14.
Beware lest you fall

CHAPTER 13

INTRODUCTION

The history of God's people on earth never has the perfect ending – not even in the millennium (Revelation 20:7-10). The fault always lies with the people whom God has blessed and not at all with the God who blesses. The last chapter of Nehemiah is no exception to this rule. *Positionally* the returned exiles were secure thanks to Nehemiah's wall-building; but *conditionally* they had become lax through the sense of well-being fostered by this security. The chapter deals with the important subject of separation from what is wrong, and what happens to the community and its members when such separation is neglected. It records failure of people in high places, and carelessness, or lack of diligence, in the daily lives of ordinary people. It seems sad that after all that the Lord had done for this people, failure crept in. The godly life of Nehemiah contrasts with the failure of some of his contemporaries.

The first three verses of the chapter refer to a high point already described (compare 8:18; 9:3) – the last day, that great, eighth day of the Feast of Tabernacles, when the word of God had again been read prior to the people returning home the next day. On this occasion they had read in Deuteronomy 23:3-4, that no Ammonite or Moabite should ever come into the congregation of God. The people had acted upon the written word, as reported in 9:2 and 10:28. They had been the obedient people (outwardly at least), rejoicing in what God had done and having made a solemn declaration to observe the Law and serve God (9:38). This was the scene that Nehemiah left to take up once again his duties in Babylon (13:6).

What a different situation he found on his return to Jerusalem! Failure had affected every stratum of society – the priests, the Levites and the common people. But Nehemiah, with his customary zeal, set about the task of rooting out the problems underlying this failure.

A FIFTH COLUMNIST

It should be noted that he did not start with the common people, but rather with those who should have been an example, and who had the responsibility to maintain God's standards with regard both to the temple and life in general. Nehemiah possessed the ability to perceive the problems, the personal courage to confront them, and the diligence to see the remedies through to completion. The chief culprit was Eliashib, the high priest and grandson of the Jeshua who had returned as high priest with Zerubbabel (12:10). Eliashib had made friends with Tobiah the Ammonite, who with Sanballat and Geshem had done his utmost to stop the rebuilding of the walls (4:1, 3; 6:1). Eliashib typified all that is opposed to God and His people.

For, when Satan finds one door closed, he looks for another. Hostility had failed; now he deployed friendship. Eliashib may have found in Tobiah a warm, likeable and entertaining person. Their relationship had blossomed to such an extent that Eliashib arranged for Tobiah to have a room within the temple precincts, which was formerly reserved for the priests charged with carrying out the daily sacrifices and worship. It had once stored the frankincense which typified that which was wholly for God (13:5). Eliashib was evidently more concerned with his position and the power that went with it than with his duties before God and for God's people.

Nehemiah was bitterly grieved. How often are we grieved about what is going on in the church today? Or has friendship with the world so far dulled our senses that we fail to notice the wrong? Nehemiah acted with his customary vigour, and "threw all the household goods of Tobiah out of the room". He then arranged for the room to be cleaned (today we may call this sanctification), so that the rooms could then be restored as storerooms for the items needed in the daily worship of God (13:8-9). We too have to be cleansed and restored in our worship of the Lord. Nehemiah's qualities are needed in the church today, where in some places entertainment is called "worship", and "worship leaders" are classed as artists. The very thing that Satan uses to lull the world is being used to take from the Lord what is rightly His.

Having had his goods thrown out, Tobiah is not heard of again. Surely the lesson for us is that we must rightly judge matters that arise that are contrary to the word of God, and deal with them so that they do not re-occur. Sadly, we find that we are still prepared to find a place within ourselves for things of this evil world, man's world, that please and entertain us.

Casualness

Then Nehemiah has to confront other problems. These come under three headings: (i) casualness (13:10-13); (ii) failure to observe God's Law (13:15-22); and (iii) mixed relationships (13:23-28). These are also problems that the church has to confront today.

We live in a society where it is the "in thing" to be casual. This is evident in peoples' manner, dress, and indifference to the plight of others. Sad to say, people who tend to be "laid back" are often admired by others. Our "God is not the author of confusion", and will have all things "done decently and in order" (1 Corinthians 14:33, 40). We have evidence in creation that God is a God of order, and further evidence in the fact that, as Galatians 4:4 particularly states, in "the fulness of time ..., God sent forth his Son". Repeatedly it is recorded in the Gospels that "the hour [of the cross] had not yet come". With God everything has a time and place. This also applies to the rhythm of human work, "Seedtime and harvest, cold and heat, winter and summer, and day and night shall not cease" (Genesis 8:22). It is important to realise that we are only stewards of what God has given us, and will have to give Him an account of how we have used it. In the last chapter of Nehemiah, the situation had arisen in which the people neglected to give of their substance.

The house of God was neglected, and, due to this, the support needed for the servants of the temple was no longer forthcoming. Today, God does not demand tithes of grain and daily offerings of animals, but our time and money are needed to carry out His commission in this world regarding His church. Casual irregularity in meeting together and in giving is a problem today comparable with the problem of Nehemiah's day. It is sad when the church is looked at as a place in which we attend certain services at certain times, rather than as *the church*, the body of Christ, those in whom the Spirit dwells and whom He brings together. It is only when we fully realise this, that we accept that regularity of, and care concerning, upkeep and maintenance of the building are also quite vital to the gospel outreach to which we are commanded (Mark 16:15); and that the disease of casualness will be cured. This regularity and care also extends to our attitude towards the Lord's work on "the mission field", towards the persecuted church, and towards other fields of service for the Lord.

A SPECIAL DAY

Although the Ten Commandments, and particularly the Law of the Sabbath, were given to the nation of Israel, not to the church, nevertheless the ethics of those commandments apply very much to our daily living. Verses 15-22 of chapter 13 outline the problem of Sabbath-breaking that Nehemiah had to deal with. Today this manifests itself in Sunday trading, but the problem goes beyond shopping on Sunday. Of course we do not live in a Christian society in which there would be a general observance of the Lord's Day, but that does not entitle the individual believer to conform to the behaviour of society at large.

Do we consider fully how we spend the hours at our disposal on Sundays? The time spent at meetings and travelling to and from them occupies at the most four or five hours. That leaves another twelve or thirteen waking hours: how do we occupy these? With sport on TV? Some other leisure activity? If Christians have been given a day of rest from work, which they call "the Lord's Day", let them give it all to Him in service and witness.

And does our code of dress give testimony to the fact that we set Sunday apart from the other days of the week? Some in the church today decry this code of behaviour as "tradition". But it did formerly convey to those around that some people reserved this day for the things of God. Jews were distinguished from the pagan surrounding nations by keeping the Sabbath.

Nehemiah's remedy was a drastic one: "Shut the Gates" (13:19). His action not only affected the inhabitants of Jerusalem, but also the pockets of the Sabbath-traders. It is not up to the church to determine what society does on Sunday, but believers, those who claim to love the Lord, ought to give testimony of that love, by their manner of life, dress and way of spending of their Sundays. Christianity is a "24/7" occupation! We have been bought with a price, the precious blood of Christ; we serve a new Master; and it is our duty to occupy our time in His service until He comes (Luke 19:13).

Marrying unbelievers

Nehemiah also found that the people had become lax in their relationships (13:23-38). They had taken wives from the neighbouring peoples of Ashdod, Ammon and Moab. Ashdod was a place of idolatry, where the temple of Dagon was (1 Samuel 5:2) – an idol thought to have been given a man's features and the tail of a fish. It was a figure that looked good but could not walk. Similarly, a Christian contemplating marriage with an unbeliever is looking at someone with good appearance but unable to walk the Christian pathway. As a result the Christian's capacity to work for God will be crippled. How dangerous for young Christians to look for such friendship with those who cannot walk the path that leads to glory!

Ammon and Moab were descendants of Lot's incestuous relationship with his daughters. The friendships of the Jews of Nehemiah's time with these people reminds us of how we all are affected by the lust of the flesh and how we need to be on our guard against it. The young people of Nehemiah's time fell at this hurdle.

The result of these unscriptural marriages was seen even more in the children than the parents. They did not speak the language of Judah (13:24). Deliberate marriage to unbelievers often causes the Christian spouse to drift from Christian fellowship. How sad, when we meet them, to find that conversation dries up when the subject turns to the Lord and His church, when once it would have flowed freely. God can overcome in every circumstance; however the effect may be yet more drastic in the children.

So much did these alliances upset Nehemiah that he took his most violent action yet. He pronounced the offenders "cursed", and made the people swear that they would no longer allow this to happen. He reminds them of the effect of marriage with pagan women even on Solomon "who was beloved of his God": how much more in their case (13:26-27)? Paul writes that we are not to be unequally yoked together with unbelievers (2 Corinthians 6:14-18). It has also been said that even marrying a person, though believer, from a different circle of fellowship can cause breakdown and more often than not leads to a parting of the ways with the local church.

As the chapter closes, we read (13:28) that one of the grandsons of Eliashib the high priest (compare 12:10) had even married the daughter of Sanballat, whose power, so ineffectual in open attack (compare 4:7), therefore now affected the centre of the daily government and worship of the people of God. How sad it is, when those who seek to destroy the testimony of God can influence it through human relationships! Little wonder that Nehemiah drove the man out.

Surely we too can learn the lesson given in this chapter, not to condone what is contrary to God's word. The influence of the world is making huge inroads into the life and practice of the church today. Nehemiah in his day took the necessary steps to put a stop to it all. Are we condoning the drift into decline, or are we making efforts, with the Lord's help, to stop wrongful practices? Nehemiah was able to conclude that he had "cleansed them of everything pagan" (13:30). He had previously re-established the temple duties of the priests and Levites. The fire of testimony had again been kindled. The smoke of the daily offerings was once again seen in Jerusalem. Is our witness visible to the people round about our place of worship, or are we to them some "odd folk" who arrive from time to time at the meeting room or church, though what goes on there is a mystery?

The book closes with the prayer, "Remember me, O my God, for good!" We too, like Nehemiah, should pray for God's help in promoting and maintaining His testimony. Sadly the effects of his work did not last long. We only have to turn to the book of Malachi, probably written a few decades later, to read the question, "Will a man rob God?" and find, sadly, that man would (Malachi 3:8-9).

Four times in this chapter Nehemiah's prayer included the word "remember" (13:14, 22, 29, 31). Throughout the book we see Nehemiah as a man of prayer. As a footnote to the comments already made, it should be said that a further study of his prayers would be profitable.

Appendix:
Nehemiah's Prayers

CLAIMING THE PROMISES OF AN AWESOME GOD

Nehemiah was a man of prayer, and his prayers allow us to glimpse the character of someone who in his day was "God's man of the moment". They are also an example of prayer-ful service in difficult circumstances.

Many facets of Nehemiah's character emerge as his book unfolds. In chapter one we meet a tender-hearted, compassionate man, who was touched by the news he had received of the poverty and feebleness of the Jews who had gone back to Jerusalem. He was not impulsive, for we read in 1:4 that he sat down and wept, and mourned for many days. What went through his mind at that time, the Scripture does not record. However, as we read his first recorded prayer (1:5-11) we are allowed to see something of the relationship that existed between Nehemiah and his God. It was a distant, almost a fearful, relationship (verses 5-7). But three points come to the fore for us: (i) the acknowledgement of God's greatness; (ii) the claim on God's faithfulness; and (iii) the confession of sins.

We also see in this prayer how he first vindicates God (verse 5). He states where God dwells, and uses the words, "great and awesome", to describe God's nature. Let us never forget that the One whom we know as Father, and whose nature is love, is also the same One who is described as great and awesome in this verse. It behoves us, too, in the day of grace, to remember whom we are addressing in our prayers. The Lord taught the disciples to pray, "Our Father which art in heaven, hallowed be thy name" (Matthew 6:9, AV). Our relationship with God is now on the terms of "a new covenant", and is a relationship of nearness. But we ought to have a reverential respect when we address the Father.

A CRY FOR HELP!

In Nehemiah's second prayer (2:4), we see a man who has a very close relationship with his God. He has great confidence in God, realizing that He is always on hand and available to help in a time of need (compare Hebrews 4:16). Nehemiah's actual words are not recorded in this case, but the implication is that he was desperate. He doesn't wait for a suitable time or a convenient place. The Scripture records that he "prayed to the God of heaven and ... said to the king" (2:4-5). If the king, whose cupbearer he was, became angry, then Nehemiah's life could have been in peril. Knowing this, Nehemiah "prayed to the God of heaven". Many a person, when danger is imminent, cries out to God for help as a last resort. But this cry was the normal reaction of a man who knows and walks with God day by day!

Although Nehemiah's prayer is not recorded, God's answer is (verses 6, 8) – and what an answer! As we consider this incident we ought to be encouraged. Our faith in God should grow as we recall our resources in Him –

of which Peter reminds us in 2 Peter 1:1-4. And in his first letter (5:7) Peter tells us to cast "all your care upon Him, for He cares for you".

CRIES FOR VINDICATION

Nehemiah's third prayer comes in 4:4-5. It shows him interceding for the builders of the wall and identifying himself with them. This chapter shows further facets of his character. He is a man who is affected by the scorn and reproach of the opposition, but also a man of action. The builders' problem was that they were having to use second-rate materials. And it wasn't neatly stacked for their use: they had to search through the rubble for suitable pieces of stone to build with. And, all the while, they were being mocked for it.

This caused Nehemiah heartache and concern. What was he to do to keep the builders' spirits up? Once more we see a man who has a sure resource in God. In our day, when we are finding things hard, and new "living stones" do not seem readily available for building up the assembly, are we, like Nehemiah, reminding the Lord that we are also despised and in reproach from the society around us? Nehemiah's prayer seems to us rather strange, in asking the Lord to take vengeance on the men who provoked him. Today is the day of grace, the day of God's patience with men and our prayers are to be focused on the Lord's saving power. But the day of vengeance will indeed descend upon the world, when in Paul's words, "every knee [shall] bow ... and ... every tongue ... confess that Jesus Christ is Lord, to the glory of God the Father" (Philippians 2:10-11).

We should also take heed to the *action* that Nehemiah took. In 4:9 we read that they made their prayers and set a watch. They were diligent, and, correspondingly, the

Lord reminds us also to "watch and pray" (Matthew 24:42; 26:41).

In 5:19, we have Nehemiah's fourth prayer. In this chapter he has to deal with the domestic and social squabbles that were afflicting Jerusalem. This placed him in a most difficult, indeed a "no-win" situation! Whatever he did would offend someone. In it we see Nehemiah as a man of discretion but also of great principle regarding what is right. We also see that, like us today, he suffered from uncertainty (verse 7); but having done what he considered to be right before God, he asks God to remember him for good according to all that he had done for the people. It is often in domestic and social activities that great difficulties occur; and in this case we see the even-handed action of a man who was conscious of God's Law and prepared to uphold its demands. In the church today we are to be governed by the Lord's desire that we "love one another", showing to the world that we are His disciples (John 13:34-35).

STRENGTHEN MY HANDS!

In chapter six Nehemiah is being subjected to personal persecution. The enemies had failed in their efforts against the people rebuilding the walls, and instead decided to attack Nehemiah, whom they had identified as the leader. In verse 9 we see his thoughts are not fully self-centred, but include his fellow-builders. But he is aware that he himself also needs to be strengthened – and he doesn't mean physical strength! He is under great pressure from what had occurred in the previous chapter and now from the conspiracy against him personally. How often this situation occurs in this present day! Problems arise in a church and then the person who has the moral courage to sort the matter out is subjected to personal opposition.

Like Nehemiah in verses 9 and 14, we have to both ask the Lord for strength when these occasions occur, and also that He would quell the opposition, and bring peace once more, in order that the church can continue to witness for the Lord.

Remember, O my God!

Four times in chapter 13 Nehemiah is mentioned as praying – in verses 14, 22, 29 and 31. Each prayer commences with a plea that God would *remember*. In considering the first of these prayers we have to be aware of what had taken place in the previous verses. The temple worship was at a standstill because the Levites had not been supported during Nehemiah's absence from Jerusalem. Tobiah, the enemy of the work, had been given accommodation in one of the storehouses in the temple precincts. Things were at a very low ebb, and Nehemiah's great concern on his return from the capital (verse 6) is to re-establish the proper functions of the temple. Here we see his character as one who is jealous for the things of the Lord. Having ejected Tobiah, re-established the tithe of grain, new wine and oil, and appointed faithful treasurers, then he prays that God will remember what he has done for the house of his God and its services (verse 14). Nehemiah didn't have the benefit of New Testament teaching regarding the judgment seat of Christ, when rewards will be given out to those who deserve them (2 Corinthians 5:10; compare Matthew 25:21, etc; 2 Timothy 4:8). It would seem that he felt vulnerable through what he had done, and needed some re-assurance from the Lord for his righteous actions.

His second prayer in this final chapter follows the account of his action in closing the gates of Jerusalem to stop Sabbath-day trading. Forcing the people to "remember the Sabbath day to keep it holy" would both hit the pockets of the traders and offend the people who bought from them. It must have caused a commotion! This time Nehemiah throws himself on the greatness of God's mercy (verse 22), for he would receive little mercy either from those whose pockets had been affected, or from those stopped from going round to the corner shop for a little something on the Sabbath! Seemingly feeling isolated from the goodwill of the people, Nehemiah has only one resource, and that is God Himself. What a lesson for us today who have access to that same resource! We have a "merciful and faithful high priest" (Hebrews 2:17).

In his third prayer of the chapter (verse 29), Nehemiah prays that God would remember those who defiled the priesthood and all that had been established for worshipping God in the divinely appointed way. Here we see a man who was governed by what was laid down by God in the Scriptures, and who would not compromise. He does not ask God to remove the opposition; he just asks that God would remember them for the defilement they had caused. We also have to be aware of what mars our daily communion and worship of the Lord, and ask Him to remove it from our minds. We are instructed to set our minds (or, affections) on things above, where Christ is, and not on the things of earth (Colossians 3:1-2). Nehemiah's desire was that God would be glorified in the city of Jerusalem and worshipped in its temple. We are reminded of the clause of the prayer which the Lord taught the disciples, "Thy will be done in earth, as it is in heaven." In heaven the Father is worshipped, on earth He seeks worshippers (John 4:23). Are we included in the company of those on earth that worship the Father in spirit and in truth? Do we pray that our worship may not be defiled by what we have been occupied with during the rest of the week? This is what seemed to have been Nehemiah's burden as he prayed for those who had defiled the priesthood.

Finally we come to Nehemiah's last recorded prayer (verse 31). Here he just asks the Lord to bless him. He recognizes that he needs to be encouraged, that he needs protection, that he needs to walk in faith before the people of his day, and that he needs strength to carry out the task of maintaining the testimony of the Lord amongst a people prone to backsliding. So he asks God to "remember" him "for good". Like Nehemiah, we too need blessing in our day and it is good to seek it from God on our lives. We need His help in times of need, particularly to maintain the testimony of the gospel and continue to teach the church the things that have been handed down to faithful men (compare 2 Timothy 2:2).

In considering Nehemiah's prayers, we have been able to identify circumstances similar to those we have to confront today. Let us learn from his example – his awareness of need, and his desire to maintain what was taught in the Scriptures – as we pray and seek to please the Lord. Amen.

LESSONS FROM NEHEMIAH

OTHER BOOKS FROM SCRIPTURE TRUTH PUBLICATIONS

UNDERSTANDING CHRISTIANITY SERIES:

SEEK YE FIRST BY JOHN S BLACKBURN
ISBN 978-0-901860-61-3 (paperback)
ISBN 978-0-901860-02-6 (hardback)
136 pages; February 2007

GOD AND RELATIONSHIPS BY COR BRUINS
ISBN 978-0-901860-36-1 (paperback)
108 pages; August 2006

"THE EPISTLE OF CHRIST" EDITED BY F. B. HOLE
ISBN 978-0-901860-73-6 (paperback)
140 pages; March 2008

GOD'S INSPIRATION OF THE SCRIPTURES BY WILLIAM KELLY
ISBN 978-0-901860-51-4 (paperback)
ISBN 978-0-901860-56-9 (hardback)
484 pages; March 2007

LECTURES ON THE CHURCH OF GOD BY WILLIAM KELLY
ISBN 978-0-901860-50-7 (paperback)
244 pages; February 2007
ISBN 978-0-901860-55-2 (hardback)
244 pages; March 2007

SHORT PAPERS ON THE CHURCH BY HAMILTON SMITH
ISBN 978-0-901860-80-4 (paperback)
96 pages; March 2008

UNDERSTANDING THE OLD TESTAMENT SERIES:

ELIJAH: A PROPHET OF THE LORD BY HAMILTON SMITH
  ISBN 978-0-901860-68-2 *(paperback)*
  80 pages; March 2007

ELISHA: THE MAN OF GOD BY HAMILTON SMITH
  ISBN 978-0-901860-79-8 *(paperback)*
  92 pages; March 2007

DELIVERING GRACE BY JOHN T MAWSON
  ISBN 978-0-901860-64-4 *(paperback)*
  ISBN 978-0-901860-78-1 *(hardback)*
  192 pages; March 2007

LESSONS FROM EZRA BY TED MURRAY
  ISBN 978-0-901860-75-0 *(paperback)*
  84 pages; March 2007

THE GOSPEL IN JOB BY YANNICK FORD
  ISBN 978-0-901860-76-7 *(paperback)*
  ISBN 978-0-901860-77-4 *(hardback)*
  112 pages; March 2007

UNDERSTANDING THE NEW TESTAMENT SERIES:

THE GOSPEL OF MARK: AN EXPOSITORY OUTLINE BY HAMILTON SMITH
  ISBN 978-0-901860-69-9 *(paperback)*
  ISBN 978-0-901860-70-5 *(hardback)*
  144 pages; March 2007

THE EPISTLE TO THE ROMANS: AN EXPOSITORY OUTLINE BY HAMILTON SMITH
  ISBN 978-0-901860-85-9 *(paperback)*
  196 pages; June 2008

PATMOS SPEAKS TODAY by JOHN WESTON
  ISBN 978-0-901860-66-8 (paperback)
  88 pages; February 2007

NEW TESTAMENT COMMENTARY SERIES BY F. B. HOLE:

THE GOSPELS AND ACTS
  ISBN 978-0-901860-42-2 (paperback)
  ISBN 978-0-901860-46-0 (hardback)
  392 pages; February 2007

ROMANS AND CORINTHIANS
  ISBN 978-0-901860-43-9 (paperback)
  ISBN 978-0-901860-47-7 (hardback)
  176 pages; February 2007

GALATIANS TO PHILEMON
  ISBN 978-0-901860-44-6 (paperback)
  ISBN 978-0-901860-48-4 (hardback)
  204 pages; February 2007

HEBREWS TO REVELATION
  ISBN 978-0-901860-45-3 (paperback)
  ISBN 978-0-901860-49-1 (hardback)
  304 pages; February 2007

GLEANINGS FROM THE PAST SERIES:

EXTRACTS FROM THE LETTERS OF SAMUEL RUTHERFORD SELECTED BY HAMILTON SMITH
  ISBN 978-0-901860-81-1 (paperback)
  96 pages; March 2008

EXTRACTS FROM THE WRITINGS OF WILLIAM GURNALL SELECTED BY HAMILTON SMITH
  ISBN 978-0-901860-82-8 (paperback)
  100 pages; August 2008

www.ingramcontent.com/pod-product-compliance
Lightning Source LLC
Chambersburg PA
CBHW020010050426
42450CB00005B/397